Let's Have Another

Also by Dan Coughlin:

Crazy, With the Papers to Prove It

Pass the Nuts

Dan Coughlin

Let's Have Another

Even More Stories About the Most Unusual,
Eccentric and Outlandish People I've Known
in Four Decades as a Sports Journalist

GRAY & COMPANY, PUBLISHERS

CLEVELAND

Gray & Company, Publishers
www.grayco.com

ISBN: 978-1-938441-81-3

Printed in the United States of America
1

Dedicated to Madelyn Louise Kramer Coughlin (hereafter known as Maddy) for her patience and compassion during the interminable gestation period of this book. She also stamped her imprimatur on the title. She now has four children, eight grandchildren and three books. She would like to have more grandchildren. She also has acute instincts. One winter night in early 1982, I stopped in the Headliner Saloon after work at The Plain Dealer and evidently overstayed my permission slip. I sat at the end of the bar, where the phone happened to be located. When bartender Red Pigg answered a call, I said to him quickly, "If it's for me, I'm not here." Red listened for a moment and said, "He's not here. Haven't seen him all night." Fifteen minutes later Maddy stormed through the door of the Headliner with our six-month-old son, Joe, in a basket and she dragged me out in front of all my friends. "How did you know I was here?" I said. "I heard your voice when Red Pigg answered the phone," she said. I learned a big lesson that night. I learned to speak softly.

Contents

Foreword: Sister Aurelia's Diagrams

FOR THE FIRST EIGHT years of my schooling—first grade through eighth—I was taught by the Sisters of St. Joseph at St. Clement grade school in Lakewood, Ohio. I liked the Sisters of St. Joseph. Most of us did. Oh, Sister Eunice had some odd thoughts. For one thing, she didn't want any of us to join the YMCA because we would meet Protestants and—horrors—we might socialize with them. She also took a political position. She told us to tell our parents not to vote for Dwight D. Eisenhower in the 1952 presidential election because, as a former Army general, he was a warmonger.

Nothing Sister Eunice said kept me awake at night. I already was hanging around with Protestants. In fact, I was one of the only Catholics on my first age-group baseball team in the sixth grade. It was organized by James Garner, whose father was the pastor of the Old Stone Church downtown, the bastion of Protestantism in Cleveland.

As for the presidential election, I wasn't going to lecture my parents about Eisenhower. They were Democrats.

There was, however, one nun whom we viewed differently. Even her name, Sister Aurelia, struck terror in our hearts. She had been transferred from St. Thomas Aquinas parish on the East Side only a year or two earlier. She was considerably older than the other nuns and she was tired. Sister Aurelia was tired of kids.

That's why she was a great nun. After all those decades she

no longer liked us, but she came out every day and faced us. It's easy to teach when you like kids and enjoy their innocent, freshly scrubbed faces. For Sister Aurelia, the joy went out of her life long ago.

Her job was to teach sentence diagramming to four classes— two seventh-grade and two eighth-grade classes. This is a subject that is essential to good writing, yet it has not been taught for 40 years. Sister Aurelia walked into that classroom every day with an attitude. We would learn diagramming or die. It was killing everybody, including her.

Once you understand diagramming, you'll never be confused about the use of who or whom or any other parts of the language. It is a lost art, however, especially in the newspaper business. Entire generations have come along oblivious to its necessity. Newspaper reporters who can't diagram are like carpenters with no nails.

Mentally, I try to diagram newspaper sentences out of habit and it is now almost impossible. It's almost as difficult as diagramming St. Paul's letters to the Corinthians, with his 50-word sentences.

Now that I'm at the end, I thank the meanest nun I ever knew for my career as a writer.

Always Check Your Zipper

THE OLDER I GET, the more forgetful I'm becoming. Sometimes, for example, I'll walk around all day with my fly unzipped. In some states you can get arrested for that. In my situation it can be especially dangerous. I'm still on television occasionally and I make speeches now and then, usually when I'm on book tours. An unzipped fly is a guaranteed way to hold their attention.

Once a month about 40 of my old high-school classmates get together for lunch, so you can imagine what that's like. Most of them are still driving. Some of them can't find their car keys. The rest of them can't find their cars. I'll guess that all of them forget to zip their flies. Let's face it. Guys my age need a fly-checker.

I had one and she was an absolute knockout. If you don't remember Allie LaForce, I demand to see your green card because you're not from here. A few years ago Allie was the main host on "Friday Night Touchdown," our high school football show on Fox 8. She wasn't just pretty, she was gorgeous, and she wasn't on television just because she was gorgeous. She was a terrific teammate. She was great on the air and she knew football. She's now on the CBS network. Last winter I caught her doing the sideline reports on a Patriots playoff game. She almost got a smile out of Bill Belichick. She also did coaches' interviews during the NCAA college basketball tournament. She can do it all.

Anyway, football Friday nights are hectic at Fox 8. A dozen of us cover games and we rush back to the station between 9 and 10 o'clock to edit our highlights and write our scripts. It's chaos. Half the newsroom is still working on the 10 o'clock news show, the other half is getting "Friday Night Touchdown" on the air at 11. Ninety minutes after the games end, our highlights are on the air.

I always keep a fresh set of dry, pressed clothes at the station because you never know our condition when we come rolling back to the station. Early in the season we're dripping with perspiration. Later we're drenched and muddy. At the end of the season we're coughing, hacking and frozen stiff. Remember, we're not sitting in dry press boxes. We're on the sidelines shooting video and dodging bodies. Thank heavens most of the high school fields now have artificial turf.

Invariably, I'm still changing my clothes when Bill and Tracy are saying good night at 10:59, and we're scheduled to say hello at 11:01. I race into the studio smacking makeup powder on my face, buckling my belt and tucking in my shirt. It takes two floor directors working in tandem to frantically attach microphone and ear pieces to me and, ready or not, we're on the air—four of us, John Telich, P. J. Ziegler, yours truly and a fourth guest host that changes weekly.

"Hello, everybody. Welcome to 'Friday Night Touchdown' . . ."

Viewers at home settle back to enjoy a great show, as usual. Behind the scenes, we're making sausage.

There was the night that Allie LaForce looked over at me, looked down and looked terrified. When the camera was on one of the others or when we were showing highlights, she mouthed the words, "Your fly is open." Remember, all our microphones were active, "live" as they say. That's how they came up with the expression, "live television." Anything we said went out live on television.

During the first commercial break I zipped myself, whereupon we probably lost half our audience.

I've told this story many times and the reaction always is the same. "What was she doing looking down there?" She was a great teammate.

Then there was Dick Zunt's eulogy. Dick was one of my dearest friends. He and I were partners on the high school beat at The

Plain Dealer starting in 1964. Over the years he was always there at weddings and baptisms and funerals. And then a few years ago Dick died. His children asked me to deliver the eulogy at St. Patrick Church on Rocky River Drive.

Funerals always throw me off schedule. How often do I get up early and put on my navy blue suit? Not often. Only when somebody dies.

I labored over the eulogy. It ran eight minutes, a tad long for a eulogy, especially because people already had been in church for an hour. But it went well. They were mesmerized by my words. Their eyes never strayed from me on the altar.

Afterward Maddy and I went to lunch with Dick's family and, frankly, the first place I looked for was the rest room. It had been a long morning. Only then did I discover my fly had been unzipped all that time.

I thought I was the great orator. I was only an exhibitionist.

The Harbor Inn

THE DIFFERENCE BETWEEN THE Harbor Inn and an army post was weaponry. The Harbor Inn had more guns, which explains why this bar on the west bank of the Flats never got robbed.

Slovenian immigrant Vlado Pisorn—we called him Wally—bought the legendary watering hole for $110,000 in 1969, a lot of money in those days.

"It's now worth two million," Wally said to me a few years ago.

That's a slight exaggeration. When Wally put a "for sale" sign on the joint and brought in a realtor in 2014, he cut the price to one million. When months went by with no offers, he lowered the price to $750,000.

In the summer of 2015 Wally made a deal. He sold the place, but he's not leaving and very little will change. Wally will remain as a consultant. What was the price? Who cares? Only the county recorder knows. However, it is impossible to put a dollars and cents value on the Harbor Inn. Its history is priceless.

For example, Wally carried more brands of hard liquor than any other bar on either side of the river. They came from all over the world. Even countries behind the Iron Curtain were represented. Some bottles remained unopened for years and the dust grew so thick the labels were barely legible.

"It made the Harbor Inn quaint," an observer of popular culture remarked once.

"It made the place in need of a good cleaning," a more cynical customer said.

What the Harbor Inn did not have was a cleaning lady. What it did have were the hottest bartenders in town. Every one was a babe. Wally interviewed them personally. It was hard work and Wally spent long hours behind the bar.

"My first wife divorced me after 10 years because I came home too late," said Wally. "Sometimes I didn't come home at all. I gave her our house in Broadview Heights."

Because Wally tends to condense long, involved stories into three sentences, I went back into my files and found this longer version in an April 1980 column.

When Wally, who was still married, went back to Slovenia to visit his relatives, he took his girlfriend with him. He described the reception committee that greeted him when he returned.

"The deputy sheriff was waiting for me at the airport with the papers," he said. "I wasn't allowed in my house and I wasn't allowed in my bar."

Because he was not a U. S. citizen when he bought the bar 10 years earlier in partnership with Tony Persolja, an old friend from Slovenia, he put the title in the name of his wife, Ann Pisorn. It was a blunder of colossal dimensions.

Waving one clenched fist in the air and clutching the deed to the bar in the other hand, Ann Pisorn cleaned house. She banished her husband from his bar and fired all his employees, including his collection of hot bartenders. She took over.

Ann Pisorn had the law on her side, but since she owned only half the bar, she had the law on her side only half the time. She would run the bar one week and Wally's original partner, Tony Persolja, would run it the alternate week. In a manner of speaking, Ann and Tony inherited each other. The employees she fired were rehired by Persolja every other Monday. The Harbor Inn featured a revolving cast of characters.

Such a weird relationship affected many persons beyond the Pisorn family. The Harbor Inn was the darts capital of Cleveland. Every Tuesday night—traditional darts night in Cleveland—50 dart boards were in action at the Harbor Inn.

Ann Pisorn, however, was not keen on the sport and darters complained that a hostile environment prevailed in their arena on alternate Tuesday nights. The original 18 teams that head-quartered at the Harbor Inn were down to six teams. Furthermore, the citywide team championships, which Wally always sponsored, were jeopardized. Darters cursed Wally, they cursed his wife and they cursed his girlfriend.

Ann Pisorn was basically a sweet person who made only two mistakes in her life. The first was saying "yes" to Wally Pisorn at the altar. The second was taking over his bar. She wisely corrected both of them.

In their divorce settlement, she proposed a trade. She gave him back the bar in exchange for their house. Normal activities resumed on Feb. 10, 1980. The traditional April Fools dart tournament was saved. The citywide tournament also went back on the schedule. The lawyers from the county prosecutor's office and the district attorney's office celebrated with a brawl.

Ann Pisorn never would have tolerated a few of the lads having a good time.

After the divorce, Wally resumed summer vacations in his native Slovenia. He especially enjoyed the nude beaches in the town of Fazana on the Adriatic Sea. Slovenia has only about 40 miles of beachfront property but seems to make good use of it.

"I met a girl there," he said. "She owned a bar where she served the best coffee. I married her. She still owns the bar."

They're still married. I didn't realize Wally liked coffee.

Wally's partner Tony, an introvert who was uncomfortable dealing with customers, never enjoyed the saloon business. Wally once heard Tony say to a bartender, "Don't serve them. Maybe they'll go away."

Ultimately, it was Tony who went away. He never said "Goodbye" to anybody, not even his wife. Tony just disappeared. Wally said he sends Tony's wife money. Wally didn't specify if he sends Tony's wife money often, regularly or once. Wally refers to her as Tony's widow, but I'm not sure if she's a widow or only separated. I never heard if Tony's whereabouts were ever confirmed.

In the 1970s I liked to write about the Harbor Inn on the sports pages of The Plain Dealer because the dart tournaments there became legendary.

The world darting champion, Barry Twomlow, did a television show from the Harbor Inn and called it one of the two best dart bars in the world, the other being Murphy's Bar in Johannesburg, South Africa. I didn't realize there was such a paucity of good dart bars in the world.

Wally and Steve Farkas were subsequently inducted into the Cleveland Darters Hall of Fame and the National Darters Hall of Fame in Grand Rapids, Mich.

"It was a very big deal," said Wally.

"Did you go up to Grand Rapids for the ceremony?" I asked him.

"No," said Wally. "I'm not sure they told us about it. They said they'd send us plaques. I don't remember getting a plaque. But it was a big deal, even without the plaque."

Motorcycle racing was another popular sport at the Harbor Inn in the 1970s and into the '80s. Motorcycle gangs lined up outside the Harbor Inn and raced like hell up and down Main Avenue. Mary Rose Oakar, who was the Cleveland City Council person for that ward, chronically complained to the police about the motorcycles, but nothing was done. Wally had no problem with them. They only raced on Thursday nights and afterward they were good spenders in the bar.

One night my old sportswriting friend Chuck Webster and I were working our way through the crowd of bikers in the bar when Chuck must have made a comment or given a look at one of the fellows in black leather. Suddenly the fuse was lit. I thought we were going to have to fight our way out. If it came to that, we were doomed.

Wally recalled the incident. He said a darter named Jim Wolan, who was drinking with the bikers that night, stepped between us and calmed the waters.

I mentioned the guns at the outset of this chapter. Wally had a veritable armory behind the bar, which wasn't unusual for a joint in a rough neighborhood. He had shotguns and pistols, revolvers and semi-automatics. One summer night—actually it was about

4 o'clock in the morning—Wally stacked up cases of empty beer bottles and we held target practice, shotguns from the hip.

I hadn't shot a gun since my army days, but I didn't embarrass myself. Shotgun from the hip. Blam! Beer bottles shattered all over the avenue. Next it was the .45 automatic against the "Stop" sign on the telephone pole on the corner. I put three holes in that sign that stood in silent testimony to my marksmanship for over 30 years. I don't know why they replaced the sign. It had no other holes in it. Furthermore, it was a warning to anybody who came to the Harbor Inn looking for trouble.

It was said that Wally had vast sums of money buried under the floorboards, dating back to the era when he had live music and he charged an entry fee. It's an outrageous suggestion. The Harbor Inn has a concrete floor. The first band, Eli Reddish, wanted the "door," meaning they would play for the cover charge. They made $90 at one dollar a person. The band next proposed a flat fee of $200. Wally was fine with that because he kept the cover charge. Suddenly 600 people showed up. As the Flats took off in the '80s and '90s, crowds of 5,000 were common on the west bank.

The Harbor Inn was a favorite playground for county prosecutors and it probably still is. Too bad for former county commissioner Jimmy Dimora and his gang. They held a party on Wally's second floor and the FBI wired the place for sound.

Ted Stepien:
Canadian Sunset

IN THE EARLY SPRING of 1983, Ted Stepien was almost bankrupt. In the three years that he owned the Cavs, Ted went from corpulent wealth to virtual insolvency. He believed that his only salvation was a two-fold move. He would sell Nationwide Advertising, his fabulously successful business, to a venture capital firm in New York, and then he would use the proceeds to prop up his worthless and debt-ridden basketball team and move it to Toronto.

Stepien's lawyer Kent Schneider was horrified. This would have meant the end of the Cavaliers in Cleveland and probably their eventual demise in Canada.

"On a Sunday in March, Ted told me of his plan," recalled Schneider. "It made no sense. He said the buyers were coming to Cleveland the very next morning to sign the deal. They had a meeting at 9 o'clock in Ted's office."

In less than 24 hours Schneider had to come up with a plan to save Stepien from himself and save the Cavs for Cleveland. And so began one of the most life-changing nights in Cleveland sports history.

His first call went to Dick Watson, the lawyer for the brothers George and Gordon Gund, the owners of the Richfield Coliseum. Their interest in the situation was obvious. The Cavs were the main tenant in the Coliseum, 41 games a year. It was home to a minor-league hockey team and a thriving indoor soccer team, but without pro basketball the Coliseum would lose its glamour.

Schneider proposed that the Gunds buy both Nationwide

Advertising and the Cavs from Stepien. The Cavs were worthless. In fact, they had a negative value because of the guaranteed player contracts that extended far into the future. Nationwide Advertising, with branch offices in more than 40 cities, was immensely valuable. But Stepien had drained it. He had sucked out $500,000 a month from Nationwide to keep the Cavs afloat. Even a company as profitable as Nationwide could not go on forever with such a millstone around its neck.

Watson got on the phone. Over several hours during the night he convinced the Gunds of the wisdom of this purchase. Between calls to Watson, Schneider had to persuade Stepien to seize the lifeline. Stepien needed $1 million by the next day or Nationwide, his golden goose, would be in serious jeopardy. The Gunds agreed to loan Stepien the million dollars on the spot. They did have a unique motive. They had to protect the value of Nationwide Advertising, which was the key to the deal.

"Watson and I negotiated all night. Gordon Gund also was on the phone," Schneider said. "We worked out an option for them to buy both Nationwide and the Cavs. In this deal, instead of being bankrupt, Ted wound up with $20 million. My shirt was soaking wet from stress—twice. It dried out once, and then it was soaking wet again."

Next came the hard part. They reassembled in Stepien's office in the Statler Office Tower just before 9 o'clock that morning to await the arrival of the entourage from New York.

"You go out there and tell them the deal is off," Stepien said to Schneider. Stepien then secreted himself away in his private office.

"So I'm waiting for them when they arrive. Four or five of them. And they were sharks. They were salivating. They smelled blood," said Schneider. "I tell them the deal is off and they went ballistic."

They called Schneider every name in the book and some that hadn't been invented yet. They were outraged that a young lawyer in Cleveland—Schneider was 31 years old—was telling them to take a hike, sending them back to New York without a deal.

"In the meantime," Schneider said, "into the middle of this comes Tom Richey, who headed up Nationwide Advertising for Ted. Last he heard, Ted had a deal with New York. He did not know what was going on and he was enraged. He thought I killed the deal. Tom was a big guy, 6-foot-5 with a red face, and he threatened to throw me through the plate-glass window."

They finally got Tom Richey calmed down. Schneider explained the deal and Richey climbed aboard. Nobody got thrown out the window of the Statler Office Tower. The sharks went back to New York with no deal and a bad attitude but with one hell of a story to tell. And Stepien's brain trust went right back to work. There were several loose ends—critical deal-breakers, in fact—and they had 45 days to resolve them. The Gunds had a 45-day option on the purchase. They still could back out, which meant the sharks would return.

The Gunds insisted that the NBA restore draft picks. This was their major condition. Stepien had traded away most of his draft picks for the next decade for players of questionable value. The NBA already had stepped in and prohibited the Cavs from trading number-one draft choices, a prohibition that became known as the "Stepien Rule." Without draft picks the Cavs were a franchise with no hope. Stepien was blamed for this lunacy, but his general manager Bill Musselman actually made the deals. It should have been called the "Musselman Rule," because he was almost as crazy as Ted.

What the Gunds were asking was unprecedented. They wanted to buy back draft choices from the league. Such a concept had never been suggested. It wasn't a handout. The Gunds were prepared to pay a high price. But the other league owners had to accept the unique principle. In order to pass, 18 of the 23 owners needed to vote "yes."

NBA commissioner Larry O'Brien and his legal counsel, David Stern, who became the next commissioner, were overjoyed to rid themselves of Stepien. But the owners' vote on the draft choices still remained. Behind the scenes O'Brien and Stern lobbied the owners to accept the proposal. Not all the owners were in favor and I never knew why. The Gunds were actually paying the other owners for the draft choices. I don't know how Dallas voted, but, more than any other team, Dallas took advantage of Stepien and Musselman.

On the day of the vote, the issue was more than selling back draft choices to the Cavs. Essentially it meant approving the sale of the Cavs to the Gunds.

"It passed, 18-5," Schneider recalled. "That's how the Gunds got the Cavs."

In looking back, it becomes clear that Schneider, the 31-year-old lawyer, was the dramatic hero who saved the Cavs for Cleveland. The Gund brothers wrote the checks, but it was Schneider who assembled the rescue team.

A few years later when the Indians' desperate hour arrived, Dick Jacobs stepped up and wrote the checks. But let's not forget that a man named Pat O'Neill put the deal together. After F. J. "Steve" O'Neill, the majority owner of the Indians, died suddenly in 1983, his nephew Pat O'Neill dedicated the next three years of his life to finding the right owner to save the franchise. Pat protected the Indians from the sharks who hungrily circled the troubled franchise. Pat deserved a medal.

Sadly, no hero saved the Browns for Cleveland.

So, returning to Ted Stepien. You know how he exited the NBA. His entry was even more bizarre.

In the 1970s Ted had been involved in pro softball, the slow-pitch variety. In his youth he was an excellent athlete at Schenley High School in Pittsburgh and he was still bursting with energy. He owned a professional softball team in a six-team regional league which for some reason didn't suit him. He quit that league and started his own four-team league. Not surprisingly, the owners in the league he abandoned sued him in federal court in Pittsburgh for violating their bylaws. This was a blatant violation of his franchise agreement. Ted was hopelessly guilty.

Ted was lamenting about this situation to anyone who would listen one night in the Competitors Club, a bar he owned in the basement of the Statler Office Tower at East 12th Street and Euclid Avenue, where Ted's Nationwide Advertising was located. Ted was not a drinker. He had joined Alcoholics Anonymous many years earlier. But he was not averse to scantily clad waitresses, which were the main attraction in Ted's bar. In order to get hired, the waitresses had to pass Ted's personal inspection.

A patron listened to Ted's problems and suggested a lawyer who might help. That lawyer was his brother, Kent Schneider, whom you already know. They had a meeting the next day that was the beginning of a beautiful friendship.

"The issue was injunctive relief, which I knew something about," said Schneider. "The five other owners had gotten an injunction to prevent Ted from starting his new league. There was a hearing to either uphold or deny the injunction. Ted wanted the injunction lifted."

Before returning home to Cleveland to start his own law firm, Schneider had practiced law in Philadelphia. He was still licensed to practice in Pennsylvania and he had specialized in— of all things—injunctive relief. Stepien already had a lawyer, but he asked Schneider to sit in on a meeting with them the day before the hearing in Pittsburgh.

"Injunctive relief is its own animal. It's very complicated," Schneider said. "Ted's lawyer was an idiot. He was going at it all wrong. I got Ted aside and explained injunctive relief to him. 'You take over,' Ted said to me.

"The night before the hearing we were up all night typing motions. The next day I got lucky. The other lawyer also was an idiot. Totally unprepared. We were passing out motions left and right to the judge and to their lawyer and in the end, the judge ruled in our favor. He lifted the injunction.

"From then on, I was Ted's guy forever. He was a lawyer's

dream. He created lawsuits in his wake," said Schneider, who remained Stepien's lawyer until Ted died in 2007 at the age of 82.

Their next adventure was Ted's entry into the NBA. It began badly. Ted was bamboozled on the purchase price and it went downhill from there.

The Cavs were founded in 1970 by Nick Mileti and in 1976 they peaked both artistically and financially. By the late 1970s they were losing $700,000 a year. This, by the way, was typical of the NBA. Those were not good times for pro basketball. Half the teams in the NBA were losing money. Attendance was dismal and TV revenue was a pittance. The rival ABA had dissolved in 1976. Mileti owned 37 percent of the Cavs and he wanted out.

Along came a fellow named Lou Mitchell, of Columbus, who had the pro basketball bug. In the spring of 1980 Mitchell bought Mileti's 37 percent for $1 million, which was a bonanza for Nick. Then Mitchell looked at the books. Mitchell didn't need an accountant. He needed a cardiologist. He almost had a heart attack. The Cavs were a financial disaster. Mitchell wanted to back out of the deal but he had signed the papers. Mileti, however, being the good fellow that he was, offered a solution. Mileti's cousin, Joe Zingale, bought a 30-day option to buy Mitchell's 37 percent for the same $1 million. Mitchell would walk away clean if Zingale exercised his option within 30 days, which is exactly what happened.

In the nick of time, like a knight on a white horse, Stepien appeared on the horizon. It must have been a clear, bright day because Zingale saw him coming. Oddly, the price tag of $1 million increased overnight to $2 million and Ted couldn't grab the pen fast enough.

On April 12, 1980, Ted Stepien paid $2 million for stock that had been sold twice within a month for half of that. In less than a month Nick Mileti made $1 million and his cousin Joe Zingale made $1 million.

Schneider sat down with Ted and explained the ground rules to him.

"I tried to make it clear to Ted that he was a stockholder only," said Schneider. "He owned 37 percent of the stock. He wasn't running the team. I talked to him for 90 minutes. I told him not to comment on the team or the management."

The headline in the paper the next day said, "Ted would fire general manager Ron Hrovat."

"I knew right then I had a tiger by the tail," said Schneider.

Actually, firing Hrovat was not a bad idea, except that Ted had no right to make such a promise. A first-year—and only-year—general manager, Hrovat was trading draft choices helter-skelter. He traded away two first-rounders, a second and three thirds. He also received a first-rounder in a trade. He actually started that lunacy.

However, Hrovat's biggest gaffe involved a retired player—Wilt Chamberlain. Wilt had been retired for six years but still talked of returning and he considered signing with the Cavaliers because of his warm relationship with Cavs coach Stan Albeck. Mileti told Hrovat to personally deliver a contract to Chamberlain at his palatial gated home in Bel Air, California. Chamberlain, however, was not at home, so Hrovat stuck the contract in the gate. When Wilt arrived home he found the contract scattered all over his grounds.

"I'm not signing with anybody who does business like that," said Chamberlain. That was the last anybody heard from Chamberlain. He resumed working on his first 20,000.

In the meantime, Stepien still needed approval from the NBA to become the Cavs' single biggest stockholder. The NBA still had standards.

In June 1980, Stepien, his lawyer Schneider and his confidant Joe DeGrandis trotted up to New York to meet the commissioner, Larry O'Brien, and the NBA lawyer David Stern.

"I'll never forget it. I got a bright new suit. I called it my NBA suit," recalled Schneider. "We go up to the NBA headquarters. Larry O'Brien sat on one side of a long table. We sat opposite him—Ted, DeGrandis, me and David Stern."

Not many people were more charming and amiable than

Larry O'Brien. He was head of the National Democratic Party in the 1970s when the Watergate plumbers broke into his office, leading to the demise of Richard Nixon. Ted Stepien's demise almost started in O'Brien's office, as well.

"How's everything in Cleveland?" O'Brien said to open the conversation. It was an innocuous remark requiring a two-word reply: "Fine, Commissioner."

Period. Shut up.

"That isn't what happened at all," said Schneider. "Ted began talking. He began a 20-minute monologue about growing up in Pittsburgh, a three-sport star in high school, his life story, nonstop. DeGrandis, David Stern and I were looking at each other. We were dumbfounded. The commissioner sat there and listened. He never interrupted him."

For some reason which O'Brien probably regretted, the commissioner stamped his imprimatur on Stepien. The league accepted him. They did not have any options. Several teams were on the verge of collapse, including the Cavs. Stepien was voted onto the Cavs board of directors, who then elected him president, succeeding Nick Mileti. Just before turning over the reins, Mileti gave Hrovat a new three-year contract.

On June 13, 1980, Stepien performed his first official duty as president. He fired Ron Hrovat and paid him off. Ted's business plan was established.

The following year Cleveland hosted the NBA All-Star Game, which was preceded by the commissioner's press conference luncheon at the Statler Office Tower. Ted thought he would dress up the luncheon with entertainment featuring his Teddy Bears dance team, Crazy George's dribbling exhibition and a man named Boots who ate powdered sugar doughnuts whole and puffed out powdered sugar smoke rings.

When the commissioner regained his composure the NBA took over all aspects of the All-Star Game.

In the meantime, Ted was hiring and firing general managers and coaches at a record-setting pace. He went through five head coaches—three in one season—and three general managers in three years.

When Bill Musselman was his coach, Ted often called for substitutions with hand signals from his seat in the stands.

In a dispute with radio station WWWE (1100), Stepien fired broadcaster Joe Tait, which outraged Cavs fans more than any other firing.

"Radio announcers are a dime a dozen," he said.

When WEWS-TV sports anchor Gib Shanley asked Stepien if he could do the job, Ted began an impromptu play-by-play demonstration for the benefit of Channel 5 cameras, which just kept on rolling. It was one of the finest moments in the history of local television.

When Stepien sued controversial call-in radio host Pete Franklin for defamation, Franklin almost died from the stress of a deposition that lasted for five straight days. When he was near death in University Hospitals, I put together Pete's television obituary for WJW Channel 8 which, thanks to Pete's doctors, never aired.

Stepien never held back his opinions on anything. He believed that teams should be racially balanced. The Cavs were six white players and six black, he pointed out, which was almost perfect.

"Blacks don't buy many tickets and they don't buy many products advertised on TV," he said. "Most teams are 75 percent black and the New York Knicks are 100 percent black. Teams with that kind of makeup can't possibly draw from a suitable cross-section of fans."

Commissioner Larry O'Brien usually began every day by calling Plain Dealer sports editor Hal Lebovitz and asking, "What is he doing now?"

Stepien signed free agents with reckless abandon because he had an advantage over other teams. Because of the NBA's right of first refusal, teams could retain their players by matching free-agent offers. The Cavs overcame that by including incentives other teams couldn't match. For example, the Cavs would

include bonuses based on attendance, such as average attendance of 7,000. The Cavs were averaging less than half that.
Sometimes attendance was 1,700. It looked good on paper but
the Cavs never had to pay those bonuses.

Whenever possible, people took advantage of Stepien's foolish
spending. In one instance Stepien reached agreement with a free
agent and called a press conference to announce it. The contract
had not been technically signed, however. Seeing the caterers
setting up the shrimp bowl and laying out the hors d'oeuvres
for the press conference in Stepien's Competitors Club, agent
Ed Keating demanded an additional $100,000. Otherwise, "Call
off the press conference," Keating said. Stepien should have canceled it, but he caved in and paid the extortion.

Stepien formed a television production company called Ten
TV and bought the TV rights for Indians baseball and Force
indoor soccer games. He envisioned himself the next Ted Turner.

"The problem was," said Schneider, "he didn't have a cable
channel to put the games on the air. He did it backwards."

That led to one of Stepien's few brilliant moves. On a trip to
New York, Schneider discovered Harry Weltman, a basketball
and television expert who was originally from Cleveland. Schneider convinced Stepien to hire Weltman, who straightened out
both departments. Time, however, was running out for Ted. The
Cavs were losing half-a-million dollars a month.

Stepien also got in trouble when he wasn't really trying. For
example, he was innocently involved in a stunt at the 50th birthday celebration of the Terminal Tower. Organizers attempted to
reprise a 1938 stunt when Indians third baseman Ken Keltner
threw baseballs from the observation deck of the Terminal Tower
to Indians catchers Frank Pytlak and Hank Helf on the pave-
ment below. When the Indians rejected the idea in 1980, public
relations man Dan Fitzsimons turned to Stepien, who often
boasted about his softball background.

Unfortunately, on June 24, 1980, everything went wrong.
Stepien himself threw the softballs from a ledge near the top

of the tower to the players from his professional softball team standing below.

"How far should I throw it?" Ted asked.

"About 60 feet," he was told.

"That's like throwing to first base," said Ted.

"That's right," was the reply.

With two men holding Ted by the back of his pants, Ted leaned over the ledge and unleashed a throw over the first baseman's head. Wind currents carried it onto Superior Avenue where it hit a car.

Cavs general manager Don Delaney was at the base of the Terminal Tower screaming into a walkie-talkie, "Too far. Too far." The walkie-talkie crackled and broke up. "What? What'd he say?" said the men on the ledge.

Ted threw another one. This one hit a 66-year-old man on his left shoulder. He refused medical treatment. The third hit a woman and broke her arm. His fourth throw landed in the street and bounced about 40 feet in the air. The fifth throw was caught by Mike Zarefoss, a reserve outfielder with Stepien's softball team.

Gayle Falinski, 23 years old at the time, an auditor for Coopers & Lybrand, was the woman hit on her right arm by a Dudley softball thrown from a height of 700 feet. She had strolled down Euclid Avenue from her office at East Ninth and Euclid during her lunch hour to watch the show. She never made it back to work. She was taken to Lutheran Medical Center and treated for a broken bone in her forearm.

"I never saw it," she said. "I was holding my hand up to shield the sun."

Her husband, Regis Falinski, was outraged. He was called away from his job as a financial analyst for the Jones & Laughlin Steel Corp. to meet her at the hospital.

"How was this set up?" demanded her husband. "Why wasn't there more concern for people that were watching? It was her wrist. It could easily have been her head."

Regis Falinski was rolling.

"You would have thought something like this would have been tested. I'm not a lawyer, but it seems the promoter should have tested it. The Indians were asked to do this. They thought it was too dangerous. Ted Stepien, seeing the promotional benefits, stepped in," said Mr. Falinski.

"There was zero preparations," confirmed lawyer Schneider, who suspected something might go awry. Schneider prudently bought an insurance policy which covered all the damage and injuries.

Stepien actually tested air currents by throwing two tennis balls and a pair of sweat socks tied to a ball. They landed harmlessly on the street in front of the Terminal Tower.

Stepien sent Falinski flowers and invited her to a luncheon at his bar on the same date every year thereafter to "recall the experiences." I'm sure she wrote that on her calendar.

Ted's wife died in 1979. When he owned the Cavs he usually was in the company of a young woman named Janice, who was about the age of Ted's oldest daughter. He had six daughters. Their May-December romance eventually faded. They never married.

In the years after basketball, Ted supported those who encountered tough times. He was particularly supportive of Kevin Mackey, the drug-addicted Cleveland State basketball coach. Ted started a minor-league basketball team and hired Mackey to coach it.

"There were two sides of Ted Stepien," said Schneider. "He was generous. He felt a kinship for people with problems."

The other side was the headline-chasing pro basketball owner, whom Schneider called the most outrageous owner in the history of sports in America.

"He was the Babe Ruth of owners," said Schneider.

The Old Stadium

WE LOVED THE OLD Stadium. It was part of our lives. "We owned it," my son, John, said many years after it was torn down.

Cleveland Municipal Stadium was built in the early 1930s. The first baseball game played there was July 31, 1932, when the Indians lost to the Philadelphia Athletics, 1-0. The crowd of 76,979 was the largest in baseball history to that point.

The old Stadium wasn't perfect for baseball and it wasn't perfect for football, but I didn't know that. I was 9 years old when I saw my first game there in 1948, the year the Indians won the World Series. As a working man I covered countless Indians games and Browns games over three decades and felt a thrill every time I walked through the media entrance. I had a press pass and a parking pass. I knew the ushers by name and they knew me. When I was on the baseball beat I declared loudly, "I get in free and they pay me for being there."

In the 1980s when my kids came along, I was no longer a full-time newspaperman, I was on television, but I still enjoyed the same privileges. A phone call to Susie Gharrity in the Indians' public relations office resulted in a couple of complimentary tickets. I never felt comfortable asking for free tickets. Usually I would spontaneously pack three little boys in the station wagon and zip down to the Stadium at the last minute. From our house on Lake Avenue in Lakewood it took only 12 minutes. I still had my pass and the ushers at the press gate let me slip the kids in with me. We could sit anywhere and the boys had the run of the place. That's why my son, John, said, "We owned it." I would plop down in a seat and talk to a scout, an agent or one of the Indians' wives and the boys would set out to explore every nook and cranny of the Stadium. We had only one rule. If they went to the bathroom, I told them, "Don't touch anything."

Parents worry about their kids going downtown alone. I always believed that the safest place for a kid was the Stadium. There were no perverts at a baseball game. There were usually 5,000 fans there, and I seemed to know most of them. They were the same people every night. Among my favorites was Leonard Schur, an old lawyer with a downtown office. For years he bought one season ticket, first row behind the screen between home plate and first base, the same seat every season. He would snack on raw vegetables which he would bring in small plastic bags. He never ate concession-stand food.

"When I was young, I thought that being able to afford season tickets to Indians games was a symbol of success," Leonard explained to me.

Two elderly women bought two season tickets near him. It was like a neighborhood. People knew each other by name. They moved around and visited with each other.

Sadly, a man named Peter Bavasi was brought in as president in the mid-'80s and ruined the neighborhood. He decreed that fans must remain in their seats. Moving around and visiting was prohibited. Ushers were ordered to enforce the rules, as unpleasant as that was for them. The next year, Leonard Schur was not there. I called him.

"Peter Bavasi lost me as a customer," Leonard said. "I bought season tickets to the Cleveland Orchestra instead. My wife comes with me to Severance Hall."

Leonard Schur never went to another baseball game. The next year, the two women whose seats were near Leonard were also gone. After a couple of years so was Bavasi.

In 1993 the Indians opened the season at home against the Yankees and on April 8, the day of the third game of the season, the temperature shot up to almost 80 degrees, a hot spell that was almost unprecedented for the first week in April. Ice floes still loitered just off shore on Lake Erie. On such a day I took full advantage of the Indians' graciousness. I called the afore-mentioned Miss Gharitty and she magically made four tickets appear under my name at "will call." For once, we would actually sit in assigned seats up close and almost personal. A special day became an epochal night.

We lived in Rocky River by then and the trip to the Stadium took 15 minutes. The three boys and I settled in to watch history from the 10th row directly behind the plate. Not only did the Indians crush the Yankees, 15-5, but in the seventh inning Carlos Baerga made history by hitting two home runs in one inning, one from each side of the plate.

During the course of the game I noticed that my son John had kept up a running conversation with a tall fellow sitting next to him. At last John turned to me and said, "Rex Chapman invited me to the Cavs game tomorrow night. Can I go?"

"That's Rex Chapman?" I asked.

"And the guy next to him is Tom Gugliotta," said John.

Chapman and Gugliotta were rookies with the Washington Bullets, who were playing the Cavs the next night at the Coliseum. It turned out that the two basketball players were friends with Yankee outfielder Paul O'Neill, who put their names on the Yankee pass list.

"How do you know these guys?" I asked John.

John, who was in the fourth grade, said he recognized them from "NBA Stuff," a Saturday morning television show aimed at kids.

"Sure, you can go to the game," I told John. "But you have to make sure he remembers your name."

For some reason, I had my check book in my pocket, which was another stroke of luck. My only scrap of paper was a deposit slip. I told John to write his name clearly on the deposit slip and put the number "4" beneath it. Then he handed the slip to Rex Chapman who returned a friendly nod. If I was driving a carload of kids to the Richfield Coliseum, I darn sure wanted the tickets to be there. It's simple enough for a player to write down a name on the pass list before each game, but it's also simple enough to forget.

If Chapman remembered, I had a gift for him. Athletes enjoyed wearing CBS Sports caps and I had a brand new cap for him. If the tickets weren't there, no cap for Chapman. Needless to say, when the game ended, Chapman discovered a one-size-fits-all CBS Sports cap on the shelf of his locker, along with a thank you note from John.

Here's a really dumb expression: "You get what you pay for." That's a lot of bull. Much of the time you do not get what you pay for. But on those back-to-back nights in 1993 the Coughlin boys got much more.

Stadium Mustard

IT IS SAID THAT Harry Stevens, who became a famous concessionaire for sporting events, invented the hot dog by wrapping a doughy roll around a sausage at a baseball game in the early part of the last century.

Subsequently, the hot dog became as integral to baseball as balls and strikes. The wiener added more than heartburn. It even flavored the game's lexicon. For example, when a player shows off by making the ordinary play look difficult, he is a "hot dog." When a manager and an umpire stand nose to nose shouting at each other, they are engaged in a "beef." When a pitcher reaches back to put a little extra on his fastball, what he is putting on it is "mustard."

Oh, how I loved hot dogs as a kid. Nothing in this world compared to the old Stadium hot dogs. They were thinner and they had skins. They snapped when you bit into them. Ultimately however, the best thing about the hot dogs was the mustard.

A wiener is a wiener, but the mustard was special. You could not get that mustard in any other stadium in the country. You also could not get it at Cleveland's indoor sports venue, the old Arena on Euclid Avenue, where ordinary yellow mustard was the only option at hockey games. Worst of all, Stadium Mustard was not available in stores. You could get it only at the old Stadium.

This is how obsessed some people were about Stadium mustard: A Lakewood woman named Kathy Madden, whose three hungry sons were addicted to Stadium mustard, would sidle up to the concession stands and pump mustard into her own jars which she smuggled home in her big purse. It was good that she didn't work at a bank.

Catholics had a unique problem. Throughout my growing

up, we could not eat meat on Fridays, a prohibition that was enforced under pain of mortal sin. That was the big one. A mortal sin was a ticket to hell. When was a kid most likely to go to baseball games? Friday nights, of course. Even in grade school we could take the No. 25 Madison streetcar downtown to a game. As I left the house, my mother would always remind me, "Don't forget, it's Friday." In the second inning as the vendor approached and the saliva was dripping off my lower lip, there was always a kid who would announce, "Don't forget, it's Friday." What made it worse, I could smell the hot dog vendor coming from two sections away.

In its infinite quest to confound us, however, the Catholic Church changed the rules in 1966. Thanks to Vatican II, meatless Fridays went by the boards except for Fridays in Lent. One day you could go to hell for eating bacon and the next day you could eat the entire pig.

Enough about canon law. The point of this essay is to introduce you to David Dwoskin, whose personal epiphany changed all our lives.

As the Jewish holidays approached in 1962, David was 19 years old and was working in his family's kosher butcher shop at the corner of Euclid Heights Boulevard and Lee Road in Cleveland Heights. His father had died four years earlier and David was expected to follow in his footsteps, but his heart wasn't in it.

He remembers the night vividly. It was 11 o'clock. The Jewish holidays meant long days and nights for a kosher butcher. David was holding a chicken with his left hand and his right hand was inside it. He looked at his friend Larry Wasserman, who was working alongside him.

"I don't want to be a butcher," said David.

"I don't want to be a butcher, either," said Wasserman.

Liberation was almost instantaneous.

When David pulled his hand out of the chicken more than 50 years ago, there were 100 kosher butcher shops in the Cleveland area. As I'm writing this chapter in the year 2015, there are two listed in the Cleveland yellow pages.

Purely from that perspective, David and Larry made wise decisions. Larry became a stockbroker. David went into the clothing business, but he was preoccupied with mustard.

"I was at my first baseball game at the Stadium. It was the 1950s. I bit into my first Stadium hot dog. I had never tasted anything that delicious in my life. I don't know who was pitching. I don't even remember who won. All I remember is my three hot dogs," said David.

Now it's time to introduce Alvie Friedlander, who brought Stadium Mustard to the Stadium. As a kid Alvie lived in Pittsburgh and worked as a vendor at Forbes Field, where the Pirates played. In 1937 his family moved to Cleveland and Alvie found work with the Berlo vending machine company. When Berlo got the concession contract at the Stadium in 1950, Alvie became the concession manager for the Stadium, home of the Indians and Browns.

"When I first took over the Stadium, they had a light mustard here," Alvie told Plain Dealer sports editor Hal Lebovitz for a column in 1977. "I remembered that in Pittsburgh we had a dark mustard. I went around looking for one. I hit it lucky."

A mustard plant in Chicago made the mustard Alvie was looking for. He told the Bertman Food Products Co., the wholesaler that provided all the food for the Stadium, to get it.

"People went wild over it," said Alvie. "They asked me to sell it to them by the gallon. I could sell 20 cases a game. But I'm not in the mustard business."

Both Alvie and Hal are gone now, but David Dwoskin is still around and he is in the mustard business.

His father had been dead for several years when David sold the butcher shop in 1965, and over the next 17 years he worked as a salesman at various times for Campus Sportswear, Lorillard Tobacco and Goodman Furniture, but he always had mustard on his mind.

"I thought about it all the time," he said. "In 1969 there were 24 mustards on the shelves of American markets, but not Stadium Mustard. You couldn't get it."

In 1969 he approached the Chicago mustard factory that made Stadium Mustard and explained his plan to take the mustard onto the retail market and put it in stores. At the time they were making several types of mustard for various labels. Sometimes it was the same mustard with a different label. Naturally, they wanted David's business.

"I also went to Joe Bertman and told him what I wanted to do and he encouraged me," David said. "Joe was a good guy. We became close friends. He really helped me get started with Stadium Mustard. I knew nothing about warehousing, who was going to deliver the mustard, or anything like that. I was at his 75th birthday party. I was at a house party that his nephew threw for him. I was probably the only one outside the family who was there."

A handshake deal was fine for Joe Bertman, but David wisely had a contract drawn up that gave him ownership of the name Stadium Mustard. Until then it was not an official name. It never had a label. The mustard that was delivered to the Stadium from Bertman's warehouse came in plastic gallon jugs with a tiny sticker about the size of a postage stamp that said simply, Brown Mustard.

So, David designed a label and began hustling mustard in six-ounce jars to supermarkets and mom-and-pop stores. In 1969, when the jars first appeared on store shelves, they sold for 19 cents.

David also traveled the country persuading stadiums, ball-parks and arenas to use his mustard. Over 100 eventually signed on, beginning with the Orange Bowl in Miami, where a former Clevelander ran the concessions. Astronauts actually took Stadium Mustard into outer space. It was served on the Russian Space Station. Also at Eddie's Grill in Geneva-on-the-Lake.

"When I started, I'd put 50 cases in the trunk of my car and wouldn't come home until they were sold. Now I sell by the truckload. People order by the case off our website, 100 cases per month," David said.

It was 1982 when David left his other sales jobs and devoted his total effort to Stadium Mustard.

At last, it is time to introduce Pat Mazoh and her nephew, who, before they died, complicated David's life and totally confused the mustard legend with their own form of deceit.

Along the way Joe Bertman retired and turned over the company to his grandson, Howard, who had a problem. He gambled. Worse, he gambled with the company's money. He stopped paying the bills. In 1982 the Chicago mustard plant canceled its contract with Bertman.

Faced with this crisis, Joe Bertman fired his grandson and asked his daughter, Pat Mazoh, to take over the business. She found a mustard plant in Springfield, Ohio, that makes a similar mustard. It's close, but it's not the same. The new mustard, made by the Woeber Mustard Co., includes sugar and more sodium in its recipe, but most people can't tell the difference.

Bertman began calling their new mustard "Original Bertman Ballpark Mustard." This is the mustard you have been getting at Indians games since 1983. Bertman's daughter switched the mustard and told nobody.

When the late Plain Dealer columnist Jim Parker pressed her about it in 1983, she claimed it was the same mustard that had been at the Stadium since 1950. Parker checked with a fellow named Bob Hreha, who by then was in charge of concessions at the Stadium.

"Sometime last fall I noticed that the mustard was a lot spicier, stronger," Hreha told Parker. "I don't think it is the same mustard we had before."

Pat Mazoh actually admitted that was true, but it was easily explained.

"My father is always interested in quality. This is the new, improved, Original Bertman Ballpark Mustard," Mazoh insisted to Parker.

Parker left it at that. He could sniff out a lie with the best of them and he figured his readers could, too.

None of this affected David Dwoskin's relationship with the original manufacturer of Stadium Mustard. While Stadium Mustard's standing in the community is higher than ever, he doesn't understand why the Indians refuse to carry it. Several years ago he had an interview with the Indians' concessionaire.

"They told me Pat Mazoh told them Bertman's was the original and that I was lying," said David.

She was grossly deceitful, but the Indians bought it.

Periodically someone in the media will poke around, but most of the central figures are now dead. Most of them except for David Dwoskin, who is now in his 70s. For that reason he has letters affirming his version, such as one from Mitchell Hefter, vice-president of sales for the Chicago manufacturer. He sums it up this way: "When we stopped doing business with Bertman and started doing business with you, we did not change the formula and have continued this product up to the present time.

"Therefore, all the claims about the Bertman 'Ball Park' Mustard being the original product can't be true.

"Our product was the original and we have not sold Stadium Mustard to anyone but you, and have not made any since 1982 for the Bertman Company."

It would seem that the Indians should turn to instant replay and review their own mustard history.

In the meantime, David has been honored in many ways. He was inducted into the Cleveland Heights High School Hall of Fame, for instance.

"It's all because of mustard," he told me. "High school was a nightmare for me. I was dyslexic. I could not read. I can't remember a year when I didn't go to summer school. My homeroom teacher asked me what I want to be when I graduate. 'Under 20,' I said."

In the end he proved he could cut the mustard.

Don King and Richie Giachetti

IF YOU ASKED ME, I would say the best beat in sports was boxing, because you didn't really need to be a great reporter or even a hard worker. All you had to do was pay attention. Boxing brought out the worst in people, many of whom were born to be villains, and they made great stories.

I once caught boxing trainer Richie Giachetti in a philosophical moment.

"Donald King always told me one thing," Richie was saying. "He said don't fall in love with the fighter because he'll break your heart."

Elliott H. Harvith, who many years ago published a boxing scandal sheet out of Detroit and who also managed and booked fighters, complained once about a heavyweight he had groomed. When he was on the verge of making a few dollars for himself and for Harvith, the heavyweight was mortally stabbed by his estranged wife. It goes without saying that this heavyweight must have been married to a very tough woman.

"The bum double-crossed me," lamented Harvith. "I always told him not to take a fight without talking to me first."

That brings us back to Don King and Richie Giachetti, who teamed up to conquer the boxing world and then turned on each other amid death threats and hit men. Let's return to those glorious days of yesteryear. Cue the music. The year is 1972.

Don King had only recently been released from the Marion Correctional Institution after serving four years on a manslaughter rap for stomping to death a small-time numbers runner named Sammy Garrett. He was looking around for a new business, a fresh start. He had enjoyed a thriving career in the rackets, mainly the numbers game, but he had been arrested, shot and wounded twice and his house had been bombed. The stress was getting to him.

"I decided to go into the legitimate business world where the real villains are," King quipped within earshot of a reporter.

It was a good line and it inspired the eavesdropping reporter to contact Cleveland's leading racketeer, Alex "Shondor" Birns, who at the time was still alive.

"He'll never make it going straight," said Birns. "He's going to fall on his face. I'll bet he flops big and comes hurrying back to the streets."

Shondor was wrong. In the first place, he made the mistake of starting his own car which was wired for a bomb, compliments of his underworld rival Danny Greene. Bits and pieces of Shondor were scattered over the West 25th Street and Detroit Avenue neighborhood, with a testicle landing on the front steps of St. Malachi Church. As for King, Shondor missed by a mile.

King surveyed the landscape and observed that the most famous black man in the world was American boxer Muhammad Ali. But something was wrong. Ali, a strident Muslim, made his money fighting for Madison Square Garden and sometimes for promoter Bob Arum. Ali was working for a bunch of white guys. There wasn't a black branch on any of those money trees, which King persuasively pointed out to Ali's manager, Herbert Muhammad, one of America's most prominent Muslims. Herbert Muhammad managed Ali's boxing and business affairs and he agreed with King's point of view. He said he would throw some of Ali's business in King's direction.

Suddenly, King was a boxing promoter. Ali agreed to box an exhibition at the old Cleveland Arena as a charity fund-raiser for Forest City Hospital, a financially troubled hospital in the Glenville neighborhood. It was a nice debut for a neophyte promoter. Although Ali signed to fight only a friendly exhibition, King had the most famous boxer in the world at the top of his card.

Nick Mileti, however, who owned the Arena, refused to rent it to King because King was a felon and he didn't have a Cleveland Boxing and Wrestling Commission promoter's license.

To solve that problem, King's lawyer Clarence Rogers, a former Cleveland police prosecutor, signed the rental agreement and technically became a boxing promoter.

Next, King and Rogers sought out an advisor to actually put the fight show together. They needed opponents for Ali. They needed an undercard. They needed a ring, cornermen, ticket outlets and the myriad details associated with a boxing show. They turned to veteran promoter Don Elbaum, an established name in boxing circles. Although he did not actually have roots in Cleveland, Elbaum had promoted a dozen fight shows at the Arena over the previous three years. He also promoted in Cincinnati, Akron, Pittsburgh, Buffalo and other cities. He had no permanent address. He lived out of hotels. But he was established. He had a track record. When it came to boxing, he could do it all. He once climbed through the ropes and replaced a fighter who called in sick—and Elbaum won a four-round decision.

Although Elbaum was a well-known name, he was not known to King and Rogers. Considering King's background in the rackets, he trusted nobody. They needed somebody they trusted to keep an eye on Elbaum.

A man named John Giachetti, whom everybody called "Uncle John," was recommended. For decades this beloved, warm-hearted man with an impeccable reputation trained a stable of amateur boxers for the Golden Gloves boxing tournament. He knew the standards and practices of the business. King and Rogers could depend on his judgment. They set up a meeting with Uncle John in Clarence Rogers' downtown law office. At the appointed time, however, Uncle John did not show up. His nephew did. Richie Giachetti barged into the office.

"He was wearing overalls and he was covered in grease and dirt. He had just come from his automobile body shop," Rogers told me years later. "He said he was the guy who knew boxing, not his uncle."

Rogers smiled at the memory, almost with amusement, but not quite.

"That's how it began," Rogers said.

So, they had Elbaum to put the show together, they had Richie Giachetti to keep an eye on Elbaum, and years later when this saga ended, the FBI was keeping an eye on both King and Giachetti. Remember, this is boxing. The last thing the referee says before the bell rings is, "Defend yourselves at all times."

Well, the fight show took place on Aug. 28, 1972, a day that lives in infamy. Don King made his boxing debut and boxing hasn't been the same since.

When the show started two or three hours late, give or take an hour, Ali sparred two friendly rounds each with Terry Daniels, Amos Johnson and Alonzo Johnson, and then clowned around for one round each against disc jockeys Gary Dee and Rudy Greene. In three legitimate undercard bouts, Akron welterweight Tap Harris and Cleveland light heavyweights Billy Wagner and John Griffin all won. All of these fighters were regulars on Elbaum's shows at the Arena.

The crowd was about 6,000, many of whom actually paid. From a gross gate of $85,000 Ali was paid $10,000, the hospital got $15,000 and King cleared $30,000. That left $30,000 for the other fighters, referees, judges, cornermen, rent and all those other minor expenses, including Elbaum's fee.

Notice this little economic sidebar. Don King paid Ali only 10 grand that night. Barely more than a year earlier, on March 8, 1971, Madison Square Garden paid Ali $2.5 million to fight Joe Frazier at Madison Square Garden. Of course, Joe Frazier actually fought back and won the fight.

Nevertheless, Don King was now off and running. Within a year King had three important heavyweights under contract— Jeff Merritt, once a contender; Earnie Shavers, on the verge of stardom; and Larry Holmes, the future world champion. To train them King hired Archie Moore, one of the great light-heavyweight champions of all time.

In their first big fights for King, Shavers knocked out Jimmy Ellis in one round in June 1973, and Merritt knocked out Ernie Terrell that September. Before the year was out, however, King fired Archie Moore for what he called insubordination.

Archie should have been fired for another reason. He had a disgusting habit at the dinner table of chewing his steak until he sucked out all the juice and then spitting the remaining meat back onto his plate. He believed that all the nourishment was in the juice and the rest of the meat was worthless. Even uncouth boxers hated to eat with him because he was repulsive.

Having fired the great Archie Moore, King hired Richie Giachetti as the full-time trainer of his fighters. Richie never had a pro career in the ring, but he won a few amateur championships in the Golden Gloves and he seemed to do good work for his professional fighters, especially the heavyweights.

As the years went by and Don was traveling around the world promoting multi-million dollar fights, he put his young son, Carl, in charge of his stable of fighters. He made Carl their manager. It was a paper transaction, of course. Carl, who was a student at Baldwin-Wallace College, was their manager in name only. The fighters still remained in the King family and Don was still in charge.

By 1978 Don was under scrutiny by the Justice Department, the FBI, the New York district attorney, "60 Minutes" and any number of journalistic muckrakers for a laundry list of chicanery. Included was a bizarre heavyweight tournament tainted by a fixed fight, phony won-lost records to validate inflated rankings and secret payoffs. It embarrassed everyone associated with the tournament, including ABC Sports, Ring Magazine and the Ring Record Book, and it cost several people their jobs. Sports Illustrated fired boxing writer Mark Kram and Jim Farley, chairman of the New York State Athletic Commission, resigned in disgrace because they accepted "favors" from King.

King denied none of it, not even the bribes.

"The secret to my business is I pay everybody," he told me

once. "When I eat, everybody eats. If a guy has influence over somebody, I'd pay him. If you can talk him into fighting for me, I'd cut you in."

The investigations and allegations went on for years, but King beat the rap every time. His honesty was refreshing.

"Catching comes before hanging," Don proclaimed confidently. "Most crooks are crooks because they don't want to work. If I'm a crook, then I'm the hardest-working crook."

With all this going on, Don felt he should have another layer of separation between him and his fighters. There was an old rule, usually ignored, that a fighter's manager and his promoter should not be the same person because these people have conflicting interests. The manager looks out for his fighter. The promoter looks out for himself. At least, that's how it should work.

So Don removed his son, Carl, from the manager's role and promoted Richie to the additional duty of manager. Once again, this was a piece of paper, nothing more. But that's not how Richie saw it.

"Richie Giachetti," King said to me once, "was my biggest mistake. He was never a partner. He was an employee. He got paid for everything he did. I always thought he would be beholden to me. I got Richie out of a body shop in Cleveland. We became friends. I kept Richie on hold, bringing him with me, paying his expenses, taking care of him. His job was to carry the water bucket and the towel and wipe off the fighters' faces. He thought he should be executive vice-president of Don King Enterprises."

Richie's perspective varies somewhat.

"I gave him credibility with white people," Richie said.

The claim is preposterous but it cannot be disputed that Richie had come a long way from Uniontown, Pennsylvania. He moved to Cleveland in 1957, fresh out of high school, like many young men from the coal mining towns of western Pennsylvania. Cleveland had jobs. It was still an economic metropolis. Richie went to work at the old Carling Brewery. Later he opened an auto body shop on Union Avenue. In 1964 he moved his body shop to West 103rd Street and Lorain Avenue. He soon added another building across the street. In 1969 he built a transmission shop. His business was growing. In Richie's neighborhood most people seemed to drive old cars that always broke down.

He also got into stock car racing at Cloverleaf and Lorain County speedways. By 1968 he was in the big time, entering a car that finished 15th in the Daytona 500. Some big names in stock car racing drove for him—LeeRoy Yarborough, David Pearson, Charlie Glotzbach and Sam Sessions. Eventually, the increasing costs of engines forced him out of racing.

Just as he entered racing with little prior experience, he broke into boxing in the same way and when he reached the big time, he took himself seriously. He was fearless and he was tough. He was about 5-foot-9 in height and about the same around. He never worried about consequences. If something was on his mind, it was out of his mouth.

So when Richie was named manager of Larry Holmes, he was determined to fulfill his duties. He argued with King about everything. Giachetti claimed he chose Larry's opponents. King says Richie did not. Richie even argued with King over Larry's money.

For example—purely for example—if King said Holmes would be paid $300,000 for a fight, Richie would insist on one million.

Giachetti contended that as Holmes' "manager," his obligation was to get the best deal for him, even if it meant haggling with his boss.

Richie recalled incidents, apparently plucked from random, but obviously important to him because he said they illustrated the differences between his role and King's.

Giachetti claimed that Holmes injured his arm a week before he fought Ken Norton for the heavyweight championship in 1978. Giachetti told King the fight should be postponed because Holmes needed 10 days to heal.

According to Giachetti, King's reply was, "If he loses, we can revive him. But we can't postpone the fight because I'll lose one million."

Holmes was a quick healer. He took the title from Norton with a 15-round decision.

The problems between Giachetti and King went on interminably and they escalated. Giachetti claimed he was there for all of the important moments in Holmes' life—trips to the hospital for repairs following fights, his wedding, the births of his children.

"Don King was never there. That's how much he cared for Larry Holmes," said Richie.

King says his fighters continually complained about Giachetti's abrasive, meddlesome and argumentative personality, and that he should have fired him earlier.

"But fighters are very superstitious," said King. "I didn't want to change things in the middle of the stream. That's why I kept Richie around as long as I did. Things continually got worse. I kept patching things up between him and Larry Holmes."

When he was working with Holmes, Richie sometimes jumped in the ring and traded haymakers with the champ in order to make his point. Richie was quick to fight in and out of the ring. He and sportswriter Bob Dolgan once duked it out in the Theatrical Grill restaurant. Richie spit in the face of boxing writer Jerry Fitch. If he had taken the Dale Carnegie charm course, he would not have passed even if Dale graded on a curve. I'm not sure he would have passed the entrance exam.

Giachetti also was unhappy with his cut of the money, his manager's share. He claimed that King owed him $1 million, his share of Holmes' purses.

All along, Giachetti had been secretly tape recording his phone conversations with Holmes and King using electronic equipment he bought from Don Myers, a local boxing figure and a genuinely good guy. Myers was an inveterate tinkerer. He devised an electronic timing clock for boxing gyms, which sounded a bell to mark the beginning and end of three-minute rounds and the one-minute rest periods between rounds. Myers was very resourceful. He could tap a phone like the CIA.

The relationship between Giachetti and King snapped clean in March 1981, when a federal grand jury in Manhattan summoned Giachetti and Holmes to testify against King. Giachetti appeared on March 18, 1981. Holmes appeared two days later.

Giachetti said he told the grand jury nothing. "I was in and out in two minutes. I took the Fifth Amendment," he told me.

But Giachetti did turn over to the grand jury three secretly recorded conversations he had with King and Holmes.

"He's been talking to the FBI since 1978," snarled King.

"I'm not going to jail for Don King," Richie said.

In addition to a little bribe here, and a little bribe there, Giachetti claimed that King swindled his fighters. Here was King, trying to go straight—he said—and he was still hounded by accusers. Clearly, by 1981 their relationship was over.

Giachetti said King had a "contract" out on him to silence him. He said he was warned by FBI agent Joe Spinelli and by two U. S. attorneys, Roanne Mann and Dominic Amorosa, all of them in Manhattan. They neither confirmed nor denied this.

Furthermore, Giachetti says a Mafia messenger even advised him not to talk to the FBI. "He said Italians don't do that," said Richie.

This spat between former business associates took a bizarre twist when Richie told me he had made provisions to bump off King. Richie said that if he met a sudden demise, he had a retaliatory button man hired to reciprocate against King.

King called such a "doomsday" machine a figment of Richie's imagination.

"He's seen too many old gangster movies. He thinks he's James Cagney," said King. "Here I was, trying to get away from the gangsters and he was trying to join them."

As it turned out, King beat every rap. He beat 'em all. He outlasted or outlived the FBI guys and the Justice Department lawyers in New York City.

Back in Cleveland, everybody is still around almost four decades later. Nobody got bumped off. Don King, who celebrated his 84th birthday on August 20, 2015, was still promoting fights, most of them for the cable channel Showtime.

Richie went on to have a brief career in Hollywood as an advisor on Sylvester Stallone's boxing movies, especially the fourth "Rocky" movie. He spent more time in Hollywood than he did at home in Cleveland in the 1980s.

Life has slowed down for Richie, however. When I visited him in the nursing home in February 2014, he was connected to more cables, wires, tubes and hoses than the assembly line at the Ford Plant. He was flat on his back and he never moved. His original parts were worn out. He could not walk.

"Nothing inside me works anymore," he said.

His main complaint was the International Boxing Hall of Fame in Canastota, N. Y. He's not in it, but Stallone is, which particularly irks Richie.

"I should be in the Hall of Fame. What did Stallone do to get in?" Richie lamented. "I lived in his house for five years. I got a divorce because of him."

When he was writing for The Plain Dealer, Joe Maxse, who was a terrific boxing writer, authored an impassioned column supporting Richie's candidacy for the Hall of Fame. Maxse pointed to a long list of world champions Richie trained. Maybe Richie should be inducted, but it may be too late. When Maxse retired, Cleveland boxing lost its voice.

King and Giachetti got together one more time on Feb. 21, 2014, at a boxing show King promoted for Showtime at Cleveland State's Wolstein Center. Richie was 75 and was in a wheelchair. His voice, once so loud and vibrant, was soft and shallow. He smiled but his eyes were tired. Holmes, who was in attendance, gave Richie a warm hug. Don King, who strutted around the ring, reached down and embraced his old adversary. That was it, a quick hug, and then goodbye.

Howard Cosell Humbled

HOWARD COSELL MIGHT BE the most famous sportscaster of all time. Just ask him. His middle name was William but it should have been arrogant, pompous and vain. I first discovered him on the radio in 1961 when he did a five-minute sports report and commentary at about 6 o'clock every evening on the ABC radio network. He had already abandoned his law practice in an all-consuming pursuit of a sports broadcasting career. He was a pro sports junkie from Brooklyn. He stumbled into radio and hit the jackpot because he was verbosely opinionated, had a commanding style and generated an abundance of hot air. I found him interesting.

In the 1960s he hitched his wagon to Muhammad Ali, the brightest star in the firmament, and in the 1970s he dominated "Monday Night Football," the highest-rated show on television. The combination of Ali and "Monday Night Football" was like a Saturn rocket that propelled Cosell's persona off this humble planet and into outer space. He became a household name.

The New York sportswriters despised his lordly manner and Cosell, in turn, held them in contempt. Some of them feuded openly with him.

Here's how conceited this man was. Cosell favored one particular restaurant in Manhattan and always preferred a table in the front window so passersby could stare at him from the sidewalk and he could feign annoyance. I always suspected that when Cosell was in Las Vegas to cover boxing matches, he would have hotel switchboards page him with messages such as, "Howard Cosell, please call Frank Sinatra."

You get the idea. Howard Cosell was an insufferable egomaniac.

So along came Jim Mueller to prick his balloon.

On Jan. 22, 1973, Joe Frazier defended his heavyweight championship against George Foreman in Kingston, Jamaica. Cosell did the broadcast from ringside for ABC. That was the stupendous upset when Foreman knocked down Frazier six times in two rounds to take the title, and Cosell is remembered for his famous call, "Down goes Frazier! Down goes Frazier! Down goes Frazier!"

Mueller, meanwhile, was a sports anchor at WTVJ-TV in Miami, a CBS affiliate. Jim, who later moved to WJW-TV in Cleveland, owned Miami. Jim related the story.

"The CBS network called us and asked if we could send someone down to Jamaica. All they wanted was a sound bite from each one that they could use the next day on the CBS evening news. Cameraman Bob Jackson and I were chosen to go. Since it was a last-minute decision, we needed the help of Angelo Dundee, who lived in Miami and was a friend of the station, to help us get credentials for the fight and a place to stay," Jim said.

Dundee, who was Muhammad Ali's trainer, had no direct involvement with that fight, but he was revered by everyone in the boxing community. He could open doors where none existed. He satisfied all their needs. He arranged lodging and credentials and said he would help them get interviews after the fight.

"Well, after that huge upset all hell broke loose in the aftermath," Mueller continued. "When we got to Foreman's dressing room it was a mob scene, so we decided to go get Frazier first and then come back to get George. We were able to get a word with Joe but it took a while, and when we made it back to Foreman's we found out that he had already returned to his hotel, so we headed back there.

"Thanks to Angelo, we knew what room Foreman was in. By now, it was well after midnight. We got off the elevator only to find a heated conversation going on between Howard Cosell and a huge guy standing in the doorway of Foreman's suite. Cosell was trying to get in and talk to Foreman but the big guy was not letting him in. We were standing behind in the hallway taking this all in when another big guy in the room looked outside and saw us and quickly motioned for us to come forward. He said we could come right in, that the new champ would see us. Well, Cosell went nuts as we made our way past him and into the room and the door was closed behind us.

"I asked the guy why he let us in, and he said because when the group passed through Miami on the way to Jamaica they had seen me predict on the air that Foreman would win. I made that prediction only because everybody else was picking Frazier and I decided to create a little controversy. It didn't hurt a bit, as I found out later, that Dundee had called ahead and told them to look for us. They took us right into the room where George was propped up on the bed talking on the phone with his wife. He waved us in and when he hung up he gave us a great interview. When we left, Cosell was still raising hell.

"The next morning we flew back to Miami and Cosell was on the plane—in first class, of course, and we were in coach. As we walked down the narrow aisle past him, Cosell gave us quite the stare.

"Upon arrival in Miami, we had to go through customs. We were behind Cosell's party in the line but one of the customs agents spotted us and said, 'Jim, you guys come right up over here and we'll get you through in a hurry.' That sent Cosell into another frenzy. We could hear him saying, who the hell are those guys?"

Down goes Cosell!

It was a good trip to Jamaica for many people. Certainly it was good for Foreman, the classic underdog who smote the world champion. And it was a triumph for Mueller, who, without even trying, humbled the most prideful sack of helium in broadcasting.

"Hold on for one second," Mueller interrupts. "It wasn't all that good. The next day we sent our tape off to New York. We had the Frazier bite and the great interview with Foreman, maybe the best Foreman interview from the entire event. And nobody in the United States saw any of it. That day Lyndon Johnson died. The news shows were loaded with LBJ stories. There was no room for Foreman and Frazier that day."

The Sweet Science
Ain't Sweet

THE FIRST TIME I saw a fighter get his face sewn back together was at a boxing show in the St. Edward High School gym in 1952, put on by the Father's Club. Many of the fighters were amateurs from the Golden Gloves but some were beginning professionals. Actually, they were all pros because even the Golden Gloves kids were paid about $25, which was good dough back in 1952.

They worked hard for their money. Nobody looked for a soft spot on the canvas. After one particular crowd-pleaser, the loser headed to the locker room with blood streaming down his face from a gash somewhere near his left eye. I was right on his heels. Because fighters used the freshman locker room—my freshman locker room—I felt quite at home traipsing back and forth between the locker room and ringside.

The doctor was waiting for the wounded warrior with his little bag of tricks, which included needle and thread. The fighter was a little fellow. He leaned against a locker standing up and the doctor moved in close. The lighting was poor—it was a high school locker room, for Pete's sake—and the doctor squinted as he stitched up the cut.

Soon my own eyes were frozen hypnotically on the needle going in and out of the fighter's eyelid. The fighter never whimpered but I grew dizzy and faint and looked away before I took a nose dive on the locker room floor. I was one suture away from embarrassing myself and becoming the next patient.

For a future boxing writer, that was an inauspicious introduction to the sweet science.

Boxing is the most cruel and unforgiving sport. I don't know why I'm drawn to it. Probably for the same reason Spaniards enjoy their bullfights and the ancient Romans filled the Coliseum to see gladiators battle to the death.

Saying this reminds me of the Sugar Ray Robinson-Jimmy Doyle welterweight championship bout at the old Cleveland Arena on June 24, 1947. Sugar Ray, who was considered the greatest fighter in the history of the world to that point, was the reigning welterweight champion and was at the apex of his prowess. His record at the time was 79-1, the only loss a 10-round decision to Jake LaMotta, whom Sugar Ray defeated five other times.

Franklin "Whitey" Lewis, the acerbic sports editor of the afternoon Cleveland Press, wrote of the mismatch that "they better have the ambulance waiting" for Doyle.

If the ambulance was literally parked outside on Euclid Avenue, it wasn't a wasted trip. Robinson knocked out Doyle in the eighth round and Jimmy never woke up. He was rushed to St. Vincent Charity Hospital where he died overnight. If Sugar Ray was distraught about the tragedy, he kept it to himself. He did not lose again until 1951, having stretched his unbeaten streak to eight years.

By the 1960s I was covering boxing regularly for The Plain Dealer and one of my favorites was middleweight Doyle Baird, a true gentleman of the game despite a background that disputes such a claim. The son of a Protestant minister, Baird was born in Akron, where he has spent his entire life except when he was away in prison. His years behind bars were not wasted, however. Known as a tough street fighter as a youth, Baird learned the rudiments of boxing at Mansfield Reformatory where he served time for manslaughter. Boxing promoter Don Elbaum discovered him in an amateur boxing tournament after he was paroled. Through careful matchmaking over four years, Elbaum maneuvered him to the threshold of a middleweight championship bout. Baird had fought a disputed draw with Nino Benvenuti and defeated Don Fullmer. A victory over Emile Griffith was the final test.

What a test it was. Although Griffith and Baird were the same age, 31, Griffith had twice as many fights. Griffith had won and lost both the welterweight and middleweight titles before Baird turned pro. Each killed a man. Baird knocked out a man in a parking lot fight in Akron, leaving him to die under the wheels of a car. Griffith killed Benny "Kid" Paret in the ring when he regained the welterweight crown with a brutal 12th-round knockout on March 24, 1962, in Madison Square Garden.

Griffith and Baird met on Jan. 28, 1970, before 7,000 fans at the old Arena. Boxing, unfortunately, does not grade on a curve. Griffith, one of the premier fighters of his era, had too much for Doyle, who lost a unanimous 10-round decision that ended with a standing ovation for both fighters.

Afterward I interviewed Doyle as he lay on his stomach on a trainer's table in his tiny locker room. He had a nasty gash in his right eyelid. He always was a bleeder. The skin above and around his eyes was marked by scar tissue, souvenirs of several wars.

"What hurt me," Doyle said, "was a body shot in the second round. I had never been hit that hard. I never recovered. I could never get my breath after that."

Once he reached his locker room, he could not stand up. Doyle's aching body sought the solace and comfort of a flat surface. As Muhammad Ali once said about fighting Joe Frazier, this was the closest thing to death.

But Doyle never retreated. He continued to force the fight, as he always did, and it turned out to be one of the last great battles in the Arena. The John Griffin-Billy Wagner slugfest and the Ted Gullick-Ray Anderson encounter are in that category. Not long ago I watched the entire Griffith-Baird fight on grainy black-and-white film, 45 years after the fact, looking for that body punch, but I could not find it because Griffith landed so many body punches, each one sending agonizing pain through Doyle's body. But Doyle never quit and it became a classic.

Doyle later went to work for the Akron Beacon Journal as

a circulation truck driver. It took him months to recover from Griffith's body blow, but to this day he says he misses the fight game. He loved it all, the exhilaration and the pain. Who's to say he isn't in better shape today than the Beacon Journal?

Another fighter who famously sacrificed his body for fame and fortune was Chuck Wepner, who lost to Muhammad Ali on March 24, 1975, at the Richfield Coliseum. In his glorious 20-year career Ali fought and defeated every ranking heavyweight in the world. By 1975 Ali was fighting every three months and needed somebody for the first quarter of the year.

Promoter Don King found Wepner, a liquor salesman from Bayonne, New Jersey, and two things happened. Wepner took a terrible beating and then became the inspiration for moviemaker Sylvester Stallone's "Rocky" series.

For 15 rounds Ali used Wepner for target practice, but the man known as the "Bayonne Bleeder" never quit. In the ninth round Ali tumbled to the canvas and Wepner momentarily thought he was on his way to a titanic upset. It was ruled a knockdown, but closer reviews indicated that Wepner was standing on Ali's foot and the champion lost his balance. Other than that, Wepner lost every round and was deprived of the distinction of at least going the distance with the champion when the referee stopped the fight with 19 seconds left in the 15th and final round.

I had to search for Wepner after the fight. There was no post-fight press conference for him. Finally I found him in his shower room. Wepner was fully dressed in a three-piece suit, but his suit coat was open, his vest was unbuttoned, he was not wearing a tie, and he was standing over the drain in his shower vomiting. Actually, nothing was coming up. He was shaking violently with the dry heaves. He responded to my questions, in between retching, but for the life of me, I don't remember what he said.

*   *   *

On the other hand, Ali was on the receiving end in his first fight with Joe Frazier on March 8, 1971. Frazier won a narrow 15-round decision and both ended up in the hospital. Ali was dispatched immediately to the hospital. He was released about 3 a.m. and arrived at his hotel close to 3:30 a.m., where I waited for him with several hundred fans in the hotel lobby. Respectfully, they opened a path for Ali from the front door to the elevator. Ali walked stiff-legged. He could not bend his knees due to Frazier's vicious body attack. Ali could speak in only a whisper. He spent most of the next day in bed.

Two days later Frazier was hospitalized to monitor an enzyme imbalance that resulted from his muscles overworking, a condition that once killed a number of Marines in basic training.

Joe Pickens: Start of a Dynasty

ONE OF MADDY'S COUSINS was inducted into the St. Ignatius High School sports hall of fame in the spring of 1988, not so much for the touchdown pass he caught in a long-forgotten Charity Game decades earlier, but probably because he was a huge donor. Naturally, Maddy and I attended the dinner at the University Club to reinforce the importance of his honor.

We were standing in the middle of the ballroom looking somewhat bewildered because we had nowhere to sit when Father Robert Welsh, S.J., the school's president, rescued us.

"Sit here at my table," he said, pointing to the last two seats at his big round table.

What a gracious man. He's number one on many people's top ten list of favorite priests—right out of a 1940s movie.

So we settled in and I led the discussion.

"Were you aware, Father, that only three Catholic high schools in the Cleveland area have never made the football playoffs?" I said. "They are Magnificat, Beaumont and St. Ignatius."

Nobody at the table laughed.

For the uninitiated, the first two are girls schools. The fact is, however, that the playoffs began in 1972 and by 1988 every Catholic school in the Cleveland area that had a boys football team had qualified at least once except St. Ignatius and Chanel—later known as St. Peter Chanel. Eventually, Chanel did make it to the playoffs six times and even won a state championship before going out of business.

Little did I realize what my attempt at humor would unleash. At that very moment St. Ignatius had a young quarterback approaching 6 feet, 4 inches tall who would change high school football in Ohio forever.

Coach Chuck Kyle and offensive coordinator Nick Restifo were drawing pass patterns and blocking schemes to take advantage of the bountiful talents of Joe Pickens, whose right arm launched the Ignatius dynasty.

In the fall of 1988, Pickens' junior season, Ignatius not only qualified for the playoffs, it won the state championship and Pickens made all-state. The next season, 1989, Pickens' senior year, Ignatius repeated as state champion and was named mythical national champion by USA Today. For the national newspaper it was an irresistible story, a team of scholarly students coached by an English teacher who taught Chaucer.

Kyle, who became head coach at Ignatius in 1983, recalled a conversation with his offensive coordinator Nick Restifo in the mid-1980s.

"It was hard to go 80 yards in 20 plays. A lot of things could go wrong," Kyle said, "especially if the other team is bigger than you are."

Most hurtful are fumbles and holding penalties. It's asking too much of high school kids to run 50 perfect offensive plays in a game.

"But you can score in three plays through the air. Nick and I figured we have smart kids. Fast kids. We thought we could have a pretty good passing offense," said Kyle. "Not·many schools were doing that."

In the fall of 1988 Pickens validated their theory. He changed high school football from a running game to a passing game.

"I could sling the ball pretty good and we probably passed more than other teams, but I didn't change the game," Pickens said to me last summer. "I was one player on a whole team. At the age of 16 or 17 you're only doing what you're told."

Pickens said he didn't even know what position he would play when he enrolled at St. Ignatius as a freshman in 1986. In grade school he had been a single-wing tailback at St. Thomas More grade school in Brooklyn. He must have been pretty good.

"We won the city CYO championship two straight years," recalled Pickens, who was among the biggest kids in the league.

In the single wing, the tailback does everything. He runs, he hands off and when St. Thomas More occasionally passed the ball, it was the tailback who threw it.

"At Ignatius there were at least 100 kids out for freshman football and there were 12 trying out for quarterback," Pickens said. "I had no idea that would be my position."

Kyle, however, was very familiar with him. Pickens was hand-picked. Kyle had invited him to attend an Ignatius basketball game the previous winter when Pickens was in the eighth grade. He got a tour of the school and his mind was made up.

"That was the extent of our interaction," said Pickens. "It was between St. Ignatius and St. Ed's. Ignatius might have been better academically."

We'll give him that, although much has changed academically over the last quarter-century at St. Ed's, which is now considered one of the premier private high schools in the country. When it came to football in 1988, however, there was no debate. The Ignatius football philosophy was customized for Joe Pickens.

On the other hand, the St. Edward offense was not made for Pickens or any other passing quarterback. The St. Ed coach at the time, Al O'Neill, ran a tailback offense directly out of the 1950s. His tailback carried 35 to 40 times a game. St. Edward passed as many as four times a game, but only when they had a four-touchdown lead in the fourth quarter. For three years in a row in the mid-'80s the Fox 8 TV player of the year was the St. Edward tailback—Chris Mobley, Danny Andrews and Chris Williams—because of their monstrous statistics.

O'Neill's philosophy seemed to be validated in 1986 when St. Edward reached the state championship game, losing to Fairfield, 21-20, on a missed extra point. In four playoff games Chris Williams rushed for 1,000 yards. But when Williams sprained his ankle with two minutes left in the championship game, St. Edward was dead in the water.

Three years later St. Ignatius was spreading the ball all over the field. In a typical game as many as a dozen players touched the ball. The line at the admissions office grew longer. It seemed as though every Catholic kid in town wanted to play for Ignatius. Enrollment soared from 900 to over 1,400. On any given day, depending on how many kids call in sick, either St. Ignatius or Cincinnati St. Xavier leads the state in male students. The Wildcats went on to win 11 state championships over 25 years, an unprecedented accomplishment, overshadowing Cincinnati Moeller's record of nine state titles in 38 years.

Pickens reflected on his two seasons as starting quarterback with a certain amount of awe.

"We were running one-back offenses, no-back offenses, shotgun," Pickens said. "While I was in college I realized how sophisticated our high school offense was. We were taught football at college level."

Under Kyle and Restifo, Ignatius turned out all-state quarterbacks like Burger King makes Whoppers. They included Kevin Mayer, Scott Mutryn, Sean Grady, Dave Ragone, Tom Arth, Nate Szep, Andrew Holland, Brian Hoyer and others. To use an old expression, the Wildcats never rebuilt, they re-loaded.

Since we're on this subject, I should mention some notable Ignatius quarterbacks of the 1950s and '60s. They are not germane to this story but they are not irrelevant. Tom Forrestal went on to the Naval Academy, where he almost won the Heisman Trophy in 1957. Brian Dowling was a legend at Yale. Don Pfeil also went to Yale and Dan Werner set records at Michigan State.

As for Pickens, he went from the front page of The Plain Dealer to the front of the line at Ohio State, but things didn't work out for him in Columbus.

"They changed offensive coordinators. The new philosophy didn't play to my strength," said Pickens.

Pickens was a pocket passer. Standing 6 feet, 4 inches tall and weighing over 200 pounds, he majestically surveyed the field and picked holes in the defense. Suddenly, that's not what Ohio State wanted. After two years he transferred to Duke, where he started only a handful of games.

After graduating from Duke he returned to Ohio State for law school, which was in his original plans. He is now a partner in the well-known Columbus firm of Taft Stettinius & Hollister. He and his wife live in a trendy downtown neighborhood.

I asked him how often he attends high school games to relive the rapture.

"Never," he says. "Haven't been to one since I got out of high school."

Canton McKinley's
Death Penalty

MAYBE YOU NOTICED THAT in the year 1962 Canton McKinley had no football season. The Bulldogs fielded no team and played no games. The Ohio High School Athletic Association slapped one of the most famous high school football teams in America with the "death penalty" for recruiting violations.

The entire city of Canton almost had a collective heart attack. While the football team was out of business, the lawyers worked overtime.

The city of Lexington, Kentucky, already had been through all that. Coach Adolph Rupp's legendary basketball program at Kentucky got the death penalty for a different reason. The Wildcats sold out to gamblers and shaved points when they played in Madison Square Garden in the early 1950s. The NCAA, the governing body of college sports, sidelined the winningest school in the annals of college basketball for one year, the season of 1952-53. Three players were banned from organized basketball for life.

Rupp, himself a heavy gambler, was apoplectic. He reached back in baseball history for a precedent and came up with the Chicago White Sox, who conspired with gamblers to fix the 1919 World Series. Eight of them were banned from baseball for life. "The White Sox threw games," blustered Rupp. "My boys only shaved points."

The Southern Methodist football program received the harshest sentence of all for blatantly paying players. It was shut down for the entire 1987 season, stripped of 55 scholarships and saw its coaching staff cut in half. When other severe sanctions extended into the next year, SMU canceled its 1988 season, as well, incurring staggering financial penalties for not fulfilling game contracts.

SMU was a multiple offender. It had already been on probation seven times in recent years. Ultimately, the president of the university and the governor of Texas faced a moral dilemma because they condoned the secret payments. They felt morally obligated to honor their contracts with the players and continue the payments until the players finished school, even when under suspension. The outraged NCAA felt no moral obligation at all. As Austin Carr would say, they brought the hammer down.

In the aftermath, the president, athletic director, head football coach and recruiting coordinator were forced to resign. But not the governor of Texas. SMU had only one winning season in the next 20 years and did not go to a bowl for the next 25 years. To this day, SMU feels the effects of the death penalty. Unlike Lazarus, SMU never came back to life.

Getting back to Canton McKinley, the Bulldogs were virtual saints compared to the college boys. Two overzealous boosters and an assistant coach went down to the Ohio River town of Portsmouth, about a four-hour drive in those days, and stole a couple of football players who weren't even very good. They never played a down for the Bulldogs. Based on the value of the goods, this was petty larceny, almost as serious as stealing a book from the library.

I'm sure you know the history of Stark County football and especially the rivalry between Massillon and Canton McKinley. I'm surprised they nailed Canton McKinley and never caught Massillon. Stark County football is more fun than Big Chuck and Little John.

When Massillon coach Bob Commings was hired as the head football coach at Iowa, he was asked about jumping directly from high school to college. Bob Stewart, the retired sports editor of the Canton Repository, recalled Commings' answer.

"Here at Iowa," Commings said, "there's less pressure and fewer coaches."

Commings was caught off guard when everyone laughed. "I was serious," he explained later.

That's the environment at Canton McKinley. The season always ends with Canton McKinley versus Massillon, 20,000 fans in the stands, an official betting line and a lynch mob waiting for the losing coach.

The boosters at both schools are identical. They don't sit back and complain. They're involved. They get up and do something about it, which is how Canton McKinley received the death penalty.

In the summer of 1961 the stepfather of Portsmouth players James and Larry Austin was heard grumbling that his stepsons did not receive enough playing time. James was a sophomore lineman and Larry was a senior lineman. Next thing you know, the father-son tandem of Don Iden, Sr. and Don Iden, Jr., both members of the McKinley Adult Boosters Club, turned up in Portsmouth along with McKinley line coach Joseph Cochran, who happened to be a native of Portsmouth. In fact, his family still lived there.

They extolled the advantages of Canton. They would arrange for an apartment and get the stepfather a job. There were conflicting stories about the family's financial situation. One report had the stepfather out of work and the family on relief. Another version had the father working a night shift in Portsmouth. There was no dispute that the mother was employed as a domestic. The recruiters from Canton made promises that fell on willing ears. They had no idea that they had just blundered into a minefield.

The Portsmouth coach, Howard Baughman, had once coached at Canton Lincoln and hated McKinley.

"He might have even applied for the head job at McKinley and got turned down. Whenever the McKinley job opened, everybody applied," said Stewart, the retired sports editor. "Furthermore, it was said that he originally stole the two players from Columbus Eastmoor."

Pre-season practice was well underway when the two Austin

brothers disappeared. Their last practice in Portsmouth was Aug. 25 and like a Penn and Teller trick, they next turned up in Canton. Everything they had been promised came true. A moving van loaded up their belongings and hauled them to Canton, where they set up in an apartment. The stepfather got a job at an auto dealer.

Back in Portsmouth, coach Baughman spelled it all out to his principal and his superintendent, H. W. McKelvey, who then wrote a letter to the commissioner of the Ohio High School Athletic Association. McKelvey's letter came right to the point.

"Canton McKinley stole one of our football players," Superintendent McKelvey stated.

OHSAA commissioner William J. McConnell and a five-man task force from the OHSAA descended upon Canton on Sept. 21 and interviewed everybody connected to the move, including McKinley High School custodian Jasper C. Harris.

Three weeks later a formal hearing was held at the OHSAA headquarters in Columbus, where McKinley principal Paul Schott attempted to defend the Bulldogs with various affidavits denying wrongdoing. But his pleas were ignored. That very same afternoon the OHSAA delivered the "death penalty," unprecedented in the history of Ohio high school sports. In addition to the cancellation of McKinley's 1962 football season, the Austin brothers were ruled permanently ineligible to play football at McKinley. Ironically, they were least affected. One was fourth-string, the other was fifth-string.

"The boosters did not have a very good scouting report on those kids," Stewart, the old sports editor, remarked with wry humor.

The lawyers kept everyone busy for the better part of the next year. Their injunctions and legal maneuvers went from Stark County Common Pleas Court to the State Supreme Court, which ultimately reaffirmed the OHSAA's authority to enforce such a penalty. Forty-six local school boards supported the OHSAA, including Cleveland's and Parma's.

McKinley's first-year head coach Pete Ankney survived nicely. The next year he got the head coaching job at the University of Dayton, where he became an iconic figure.

During its sabbatical McKinley played intramural football games every Saturday afternoon, charging admission and attracting crowds as large as 5,000. The sympathetic Massillon band played at one of the intramural games.

When football resumed at Canton McKinley in 1963, McKinley and Massillon played twice to recoup the lost revenue of the previous year. Massillon won both games, 24-20 at Massillon and 22-6 in Canton. McKinley's record was 6-4 in its comeback season under interim coach Tony Ware.

The following year McKinley went 9-1 under new head coach Don Nehlen and was ranked second in the final Associated Press state poll. And they did it without the Austin brothers. Nehlen went on to become head college coach at West Virginia.

In 1970 McKinley and Portsmouth finally locked horns on the football field, with McKinley avenging the unpleasantness of eight years earlier by a 44-14 score.

Current OHSAA commissioner Dan Ross has said it is unlikely the death penalty will ever be repeated in Ohio.

Bob Commings:
Fifth Year Blues

BACK IN THE 1970s St. Edward High School football coach Dan Flaherty scoffed when I asked him if he could jump directly into a head coaching job in college.

"College coaches are so farther advanced than we are," he said. "I teach six classes. I can't even start thinking about football until 3 o'clock in the afternoon."

That was true. Flaherty taught six religion classes. He had to plan lessons and grade papers for almost 200 students before he could turn on the movie projector to study his next opponent.

I often wondered how St. Ignatius coach Chuck Kyle would have done in college. After winning his first two state championships at St. Ignatius, Kyle was offered a job on the Notre Dame coaching staff in the early 1990s. He turned it down.

"The NCAA said the next year the major colleges would be limited to nine coaches. I would have been the 10th coach at Notre Dame and the last hired. I would have been the one they let go," Kyle told me at the time.

Ten years before that Notre Dame hired another high school coach. They hired Gerry Faust from Cincinnati Moeller, not as the 10th man on the staff, but as the head coach. Faust had posted a string of five state championships at Moeller where his 19-year career record was 178-23-2.

Denny Dressman of the Cincinnati Enquirer, who had just written a book about Faust, told me confidently that Faust would become one of the all-time great college coaches. Dressman was wrong. Five years later Faust resigned under pressure with a 30-26-1 record, not bad but not quite what Notre Dame had in mind.

Ever since Paul Brown went directly from Massillon to Ohio State in 1941, colleges have looked for that same lightning in a bottle. Brown had won six straight state championships and had an 80-8-2 record when he left Massillon for Ohio State, where he won a national championship in his second year. After coaching a Navy team in World War II, he became the first coach of the Cleveland Browns, where he won seven league championships in his first 10 years. He's in both the college and pro football halls of fame. He also was the first coach of the Cincinnati Bengals, who went to two Super Bowls while he was president of the franchise.

After Brown, no less than five Massillon coaches were hired as college head coaches with no other job in between. Only one of them was successful in college.

William "Bud" Houghton, who succeeded Brown at Massillon, became the head coach at the University of Akron. Houghton had won a state championship at Massillon. His four years at Akron were grim—a 7-27-1 record.

Even by Massillon standards, Chuck Mather's six years (1948-53) were singularly scintillating. His record was 57-3 and his teams were voted state champion all six years and national champion three times. It was impossible not to notice, which led to a call from the University of Kansas. The results, however, were disappointing. In four years Mather's record was 11-26-3 and he was fired. He ended his career as an assistant with the Chicago Bears.

After only two years at Massillon (1956-57) with a 16-3 record, Lee Tressel began a brilliant 23 years at Baldwin-Wallace College where his 155-52-6 record included a Division III national championship and a national coach of the year award.

Leo Strang spent six years (1958-63) at Massillon with a 54-8-1 record and three wire-service state championships. That led to four years at Kent State, where his record was less than ordinary (17-20-2).

The last Massillon coach to make the leap from high school to college was Bob Commings, whose five years (1969-73) at Massillon included a 43-6-2 record and two wire-service state championships. When the Iowa job opened, Commings, who played his college ball there, campaigned aggressively for the job. He actually said he would take a one-year contract to prove himself. That sealed the deal. When Commings moved to Iowa City in 1974, the Hawkeyes had not enjoyed a winning season since 1961. Alas, nothing changed. After five more losing seasons and a 17-38 record, Commings was fired.

Commings returned to Stark County and spent 12 successful seasons coaching GlenOak. In 1980 Bob and I spent an hour together alone in the GlenOak locker room, where he shared his innermost thoughts and regrets.

"This is what they do," he said. "Just when you've learned to coach, they fire you."

That was Iowa coach Forest Evashevski's assessment of the Notre Dame situation with young coach Terry Brennan. Brennan was 25 when he was picked to succeed legendary Frank Leahy as Notre Dame coach in 1954. Two years earlier he was coaching at Mt. Carmel High School in Chicago. One year earlier he was coaching the Notre Dame freshman team.

"I would sit in meetings with Evashevski," said Commings. "We played Notre Dame every year. In Brennan's earlier years, Evashevski said, he was not a good coach, but by his last year he had learned to coach. And they fired him."

Obviously, Commings realized the parallels. He lived the parallels. He got his five years. Just as Terry Brennan got his five years. Just as Gerry Faust got his five years. Bud Houghton, Chuck Mather and Leo Strang got only four years each.

Sadly, Commings was only 59 when he was diagnosed with cancer and died. He was one of the most successful high school football coaches in Stark County history. In 24 seasons his record was 169-66-7. The only blemish on his record was the five years in Iowa.

West Senate Memories

IF THEY HAD PUBLICIZED it, a smart entrepreneur could have charged a hundred bucks a person to watch four high school kids play a two-on-two basketball game at Cleveland's Estabrook Recreation Center. This was not just any pickup basketball game. It was late summer or early fall of 1964 and the game involved basketball royalty. It matched Phil Argento and John Petch versus Bill Hann and Lee Walczuk, the four most revered names of that era in Cleveland basketball, and they were together on one court. They were legends before they were old enough to vote. Among them they averaged 110 points a game in high school.

The official start of high school basketball practice was more than a month away, but for the great players, the serious players, basketball practice was 365 days a year. In the summer they knew where to find each other at the outdoor courts in Lakewood and on the East Side. Argento, for example, haunted the outdoor courts on the East Side, where he polished his game against older black players. I knew no other white player from the West Side who enjoyed such total acceptance.

On this particular day, however, the four legends wandered into Estabrook Rec at the same time. When summer was over and the weather forced everyone inside, you would usually find the best players on the West Side at Estabrook, which was on Fulton Road near Memphis Avenue in Old Brooklyn, or at Navy Park Gym at West 73rd Street and Clinton Avenue.

"The games were serious. No referees. No fouls. A lot of banging," recalled John Wells, the all-scholastic guard from St. Edward. "We all knew each other. There were no strangers."

The entire Rhodes High team often was involved. Jim Holland came in from the distant suburb of Bay Village. Wells' St. Edward teammate Walter Violand was a regular, as well as Brian Dowling and Bill DeLong from St. Ignatius. They both came from Cleveland Heights.

But this was a quiet afternoon. The legends had a court all to themselves. Half a dozen men on an adjacent court paused briefly to watch, and then they resumed their own game. Petch recalled that they played for 20 or 30 minutes. They kept score, but it wasn't serious score-keeping. Then they drifted off to do their own thing. And what a thing they did.

They were all guards who rewrote the high school record books with their jump shots. Argento, Petch and Walczuk averaged more than 30 points a game. Hann averaged a shade under 20 and had nonpareil ball-handling skills. Keep in mind that the three-point shot had not been introduced yet, but many of their shots were beyond what later became the three-point arc.

Argento, who played for West High, once bombarded South High with 66 points, a single-game record for northeastern Ohio that has stood for more than half a century. It is estimated that he would have scored 80 if the three-point shot had been in effect. Needless to say, there were no cell phones, no tweeting, no texting, no social media of any kind in 1964. But thanks to the old rotary dial telephone and Tom Carson, who broadcast high school scores on radio station KYW 1100, word of Argento's 66-point performance spread through the West Side minutes after the final buzzer. The Lakewood High School team learned of it moments after their own game ended. Barely dry from their post-game showers, the Lakewood players jumped in a couple of cars and drove quickly to Howard Johnson's, the famous ice cream parlor at the west end of the Shoreway, which everyone knew was the post-game hangout for the West High team.

"Do you know what we wanted to do?" Bob Wonson, one of

the Lakewood players, said years later. "We wanted to look at him. We just wanted to look at Phil. There he was, stretched out in a booth like a king. He took up one entire side of the booth. We just stared at him. That was history. We knew we'd never forget it."

Wonson went on to enjoy his own glorious career as the head basketball coach at Shaker Heights High School. Before he passed away a few years ago I asked him one more question about the night Argento scored 66.

"You seem to have such a vivid memory of that night," I said. "Whom did you play that night and did you win or lose?"

"I have no idea," he said.

Petch, who seemed to fling the ball with both hands from over his head, began his varsity career at Lincoln High on Scranton Road in the Tremont neighborhood and later transferred to West High. While playing for Lincoln he scored 51 against Holy Name one night. After moving to West High he scored another 51 against West Tech.

West Tech coach Larry Chernauskas said it was impossible to contain Petch. He sent assistant coach Fred George to scout him.

"Fred came back and said Petch is right-handed but he likes to go to his left," Chernauskas said. "So I told Mike Gelsinger, who was going to guard Petch, to make him go to his right. I said, 'Don't let him go left.' Gelsinger did exactly what I told him.

"Well, Petch scored 51. I said to Fred George, 'What kind of scouting job was that?' Fred said, 'If we let him go left he would have scored 80.' Fred was probably right."

One of the greatest single-game matchups ever pitted Lincoln's John Petch against West High's Phil Argento. The week of the game Petch was still wearing a cast on a broken right wrist, an injury he incurred four weeks earlier. The entire city had been waiting for this showdown and Petch did not intend to disappoint anyone.

"My brother told me to soak the cast in the bathtub to soften it and then I could cut it off," Petch said. "I did that and I played. The West High gym was packed. People were actually standing all around the court. West High beat us by four or five points. Phil scored 45. I had 42. I never went back to the doctor."

Hann dazzled everyone with his ball-handling and passing for Rhodes High in the Old Brooklyn neighborhood of Cleveland. His teammate Steve Christafaris claims that Hann sacrificed his scoring for the good of the team.

"Billy averaged something like 19.8 points a game because he set up everybody else. He set picks, he made pinpoint passes, he found open men, he shared the ball," said Christafaris. "He could have averaged close to 30. As a matter of fact, he did score in the high 40s or 50 one night. He could have done that all the time if shooting was his only job."

The result was the greatest team in the history of Rhodes High School. Taking a page from the Harlem Globetrotters routine, they played the song, "Sweet Georgia Brown," during pre-game warmups. Maybe Rhodes stole the song from East Tech, which also used it during its pre-game show. In any case, nobody ever got indicted for petty theft.

Rhodes won the West Senate in 1964 and became the first West Senate school since 1952 to interrupt the dominance of the East Senate in the city championship game at the old Arena. That was the season that Rhodes coach Andy Moran satisfied a lot of grudges.

"We were playing at Rhodes and they had us down by 36 after three quarters. Andy took out some of his starters," recalled West Tech coach Larry Chernauskas. "We scored three straight baskets to start the fourth quarter and we were down by 30. I happened to look over at the scorer's table and Billy Hann was reporting back in. 'Billy, you're going back in?' I said to him. Billy just sort of shrugged, as though to say he didn't know why either.

"Andy was watching this and he got up and pulled a card out of the inside pocket of his sports coat and waved it in my face. It had the scores of his biggest losses on it. Right up on top was, West Tech 99, Rhodes 48. 'You can look at this, Buster,' he said."

Rhodes won the West Senate and then headed downtown to meet East High for the city championship. A sellout crowd of 10,000 was waiting for them at the old Cleveland Arena. Steve Christafaris sets the stage.

"We came out to warm up and the Arena organist started playing 'Sweet Georgia Brown.' Andy knew the organist. He got him to play it. At the other end of the floor the East High players stopped and looked at us with their hands on their hips," said Christafaris.

Here was an all-white team going through its fancy warmup routine to the anthem of a world-famous black team. This wasn't the only audacity. Rhodes went on to shock East High, 67-57, to win the 1964 city championship game.

"Nobody gave us a chance to win," said Christafaris. "In a scrimmage before the season East High beat us by 10. That win at the Arena primed us for the state tournament."

Christafaris doesn't say Rhodes would have won the state title, which went to a great Dayton Belmont team led Bill Hosket and Don May. But we'll never know. Rhodes never got the chance.

Andy Moran had an offensive juggernaut at Rhodes. All five starters averaged scoring in double figures and the sixth man averaged 9.8. Inexplicably, Moran decided to play a slowdown game against an inferior Elyria team in the district tournament and lost, 43-42.

"It broke my heart," Christafaris said. "The moon and the stars aligned right for Elyria. On any other night we would have beat them by 25."

With Rhodes out of the way, East High eventually played Elyria in the state semifinals and won handily, 58-31. The next night Dayton Belmont routed East, 89-60, to win the 1964 state championship.

* * *

Lee Walzcuk was a shooting machine who scored 1,000 points by the middle of his junior year at Gilmour Academy, a small, prestigious and wildly expensive all-boys Catholic boarding school in Gates Mills. He poured in 31 points a game, mainly against other small schools, and his exploits were chronicled in little two- and three-paragraph articles in the back pages of The Plain Dealer sports section.

In January 1965, Walczuk exploded into the headlines. He transferred from Gilmour to St. Edward, where 1,600 boys trotted the hallways of the large all-boys school in Lakewood. St. Edward had a 15-1 record against other big-time powerhouses when Walczuk and his 31 points a game stepped into its lineup.

"He's the key," St. Edward guard Dan McNamara said to me during Walczuk's first practice with his new team. It was an unusual reaction because Walczuk had just taken McNamara's starting job.

High school basketball fans reacted passionately. Public school people were outraged. Other Catholic schools were resentful. Today it's commonplace for kids to transfer for the sake of transferring. In 1965 hardly anybody transferred. But Walczuk wasn't just anybody. He was a somebody.

Oddly, John Petch transferred from Lincoln to West High without great fanfare. But he didn't do it at midseason. He didn't play for one team on Saturday and for another team the following Friday, which was Walczuk's scenario.

As great as he was, Walczuk didn't fit in with that St. Edward team. The chemistry was upset and St. Ed's lost in its first tournament game to Lakewood, a .500 team.

None of this was Lee's idea. His father, Leo Walczuk, initiated the transfer and actually moved his entire family from the East Side to an apartment in Lakewood to comply with Ohio High School Athletic Association transfer rules. Lee, however, made the most of his situation. He continued to improve his game on the Lakewood outdoor courts and at Navy Park and Estabrook Recreation.

"He told me it really opened his eyes to West Senate basketball," Christafaris recalled.

The four legends went on to enjoy successful lives. Argento was recruited by Adolph Rupp and became a three-year starter at Kentucky. He played briefly in the American Basketball Association. He worked in real estate and eventually turned to coaching. He was the head coach at Avon Lake, Lutheran West and most recently Lakewood.

Hann was a three-year starter at Tennessee and then entered banking, eventually becoming a bank president. The last time I talked to him was in 1975. I was at The Plain Dealer and he was being held hostage. Hann was the branch manager of a bank on Lorain Avenue and West 130th Street which was being robbed by the famous bank robber Fast Eddie Watkins.

It was not a good day for either Billy or Fast Eddie. They shouldn't have come to work that day. Billy was suffering from the flu and had a fever. Fast Eddie, who usually worked quickly and left with a bag of money, ran into one snag after another.

Soon the bank was surrounded by cops and the FBI, and Fast Eddie was trapped along with nine hostages in a stalemate that lasted through the day and into the night.

During this period I called the bank. One of the tellers answered the phone. I asked to speak to Billy and she put him on. Billy said everyone was fine except him. His temperature was rising, especially after the FBI cut off the electricity, which turned off the air conditioning on a hot summer afternoon.

Eventually Fast Eddie released Billy, but the stalemate continued for several hours while Fast Eddie pondered his options. He finally concluded there weren't any and surrendered without getting a dime after a standoff that lasted for 21 hours. Fast Eddie went to prison, but he escaped and was caught robbing another bank. He died in prison at 82. Billy became the president of a bank and was never robbed again.

Walczuk was recruited by John Wooden to UCLA but played very little on national championship teams that featured Lew Alcindor, who later became Kareem Abdul-Jabbar. Lee never bought into the UCLA program because of the funny business he said was going on. He went into acting and married a Polish movie star. He and his wife now run a wedding photography business in Hawaii.

Petch was raised by an older sister and a brother after his mother died and his father left. Browns Hall of Famer Dante Lavelli recommended him to Ohio State, and St. Ignatius coach John Wirtz talked to him about the University of Dayton. But he soon wore a different uniform. John graduated from West High in January 1966. He was drafted into the Army in April and reported for duty in August. When his hitch was over Petch returned to Cleveland and played amateur basketball and worked at the Chevrolet plant in Parma as a transmission quality inspector. He retired in 2001 at the age of 53 and still gets together every Wednesday morning for breakfast with other old players and coaches at the Red Chimney restaurant on Fleet Avenue at East 65th Street.

I often reminisce about the glory days of West Senate basketball in the 1960s, when cracker-box gyms were packed to overflowing with germ-infested teenagers. High school basketball was a major sport before the Cavaliers came along in 1970. There were two winter sports in those days—Cleveland Barons hockey at the old downtown Arena and high school basketball. On Saturday mornings the top headline across the first sports page was usually reserved for a Senate basketball game.

The great horse racing writer Bob "Railbird" Roberts remembers driving from Lake County in the winter to the little bandbox gymnasiums on the West Side to see these magical stars in person.

"I was in high school at Eastlake North and we'd read about these guys like Argento and Petch scoring 30, 40, 50 points a game," the Railbird said. "We couldn't believe it. We had to see them for ourselves. And when Argento scored 66 for West High, it was like Roger Maris hitting 61 for the Yankees."

When I was on the high school beat in the 1960s, I was usually sick all winter because of breathing used air in those West Senate gyms. Kids were packed shoulder to shoulder. They coughed on me, they touched me, they shook my hands. Afterward I grabbed an Arby's roast beef sandwich with both hands. And I wondered why I was sick. Nevertheless, it was a great time to be in high school. It was a great time to be on the high school beat.

Invisible High School

MY FIRST NEWSPAPER JOB after college was second man on a two-man sports staff in Lynchburg, Virginia. The Lynchburg News was a seven-day morning paper owned by the Glass family, one of the most prominent political families in the state.

Lynchburg's minor-league baseball team was owned by Calvin Falwell, a wealthy businessman and first cousin of a young man about my age who would grow up to be a famous evangelist and founder of Liberty University. The evangelist, of course, was Jerry Falwell. I never met him. I drank and stayed out late at night. He didn't.

I loved my boss, sports editor Bill Beck, who worked for years as a hard news reporter in Washington, D.C. He landed in Lynchburg as a sports editor when his paper in Washington folded. He told me wonderful stories about the old Washington Senators and about covering executions. He drank copious amounts of whatever beer I had in my refrigerator.

I immensely enjoyed Lynchburg and my job as a professional newspaperman. It was my dream job. Furthermore, I was on my own for the first time. I didn't have Mom and Dad hovering over me. I didn't have the priests in college scrutinizing my comings and goings. Not everybody enjoyed me, however, and I don't blame them. I was young, dumb, loud and cocky. Lucky for Lynchburg, I didn't stay long. In the summer of 1961 the Soviets built the Berlin Wall and President Kennedy retaliated by activating two new divisions, one of which was the First Armored Division at Fort Hood, Texas. It was there that I spent the better part of the next two years.

I never forgot Lynchburg, however. There was much to learn

in Lynchburg. For example, there were two high schools—the white school and the black school. Blacks weren't blacks then. They were colored or Negroes. They each had football teams which shared the same 6,000-seat stadium—but not at the same time. The black school played on Thursday nights. The white school played on Friday nights. I could accept that. It was the South. It was still a different world. They had their old ways.

The week that the high school football season opened, I said to Bill Beck, "I probably should do advance stories on both schools, right? I'll cover the game Thursday night and then I'll cover the Friday game."

"No, we don't cover the colored school," Bill said.

I damn near fell off my chair. It was true. We didn't cover their games or any other events. We didn't cover their graduation, their awards ceremonies or their alumni events. It was as though the black school did not exist. I don't remember if we covered black arrests or arraignments or if we ignored those, also. Beyond the fairness and decency issue, it was bad business. They were turning down black readers, black advertisers, black customers.

Back home in Cleveland, all three papers covered East Tech's state basketball championships with eight-column headlines on page one. East Tech happened to be all black, but integrated schools had been a way of life in Ohio for years. Back in the 1930s Marion Motley played for Canton McKinley and Horace Gillom played for Massillon. Needless to say, I mentioned them because they were black football stars on predominantly white teams.

On my way to work in Lynchburg, I often drove past the home of Doctor Robert Johnson, a black physician who had a young tennis protege. High shrubs and foliage secluded his house from the outside world, so that I never got a glimpse of young Arthur Ashe.

No, we didn't write about him, either.

Won Sok Hung

BILL HICKEY WAS SIPPING a martini one night in the Headliner Bar and lamenting how his long career as the television critic of The Plain Dealer would be remembered.

"I wrote 5,000 columns and even won a national award," he said. "No one remembered any of them. But everyone I met said, 'Aren't you the guy who wrote about the Sake Bowl?' All I could say was, 'I plead guilty, your honor.' That's a hell of a way to bow out."

In 1965 Hickey was a copy editor in The Plain Dealer sports department, which is fairly tedious work, and to spice up his life he wrote an "items and oddities" column once a week. He came to work an hour early in order to scan the wires for off-beat stuff that otherwise would never get in the paper. To show you where Hickey's inspiration came from, the title of his column was "This Sporting Life," which also was the title of a Richard Harris movie about a drunken rugby player.

The wires were not bottomless wells of material, however, so to keep himself interested he created Pusan State University in South Korea and its star football player, Won Sok Hung. It began with one sentence about a 4-foot-11, 137-pound running back and climaxed with the Sake Bowl in Tokyo for the championship of the entire Asian Land Mass.

Hickey sucked us in like the winner of a walleye fishing tournament.

Tucked in the middle of a column was one sentence, "Won Sok Hung churned up the turf at MacArthur Stadium for 396 yards as the Pusan State Panthers ran roughshod over the Seoul Spartans in a Korean Big Ten game Saturday."

"I thought it was a one-shot thing," Hickey said, "but the reaction was immediate and I knew then where it was going."

In the first place, readers were surprised to learn that colleges in Korea played football, which they do not. They were further amazed that a little man less than 5 feet tall and weighing barely more than Audrey Hepburn, a big movie star of the day, could rush for almost 400 yards in a single game. Readers wanted more of it and Hickey complied. Each week, he recounted more spectacular tales from Asian football and introduced more characters. Plain Dealer readers were absolutely captivated and, best of all, they could get this story only in Ohio's largest morning paper.

Hickey would sit at the bar of the Headliner, which was one short block from the front door of The Plain Dealer on Superior Avenue, drinking martinis and writing notes in an official reporter's notebook. He made a list of characters as though he were making out the starting lineup. He wrote the name of coach Noo Rok Nee, known as the "Old Fox," quarterback Kim Dip Thong and linebacker Won Dum Jok, the meanest man in all of Korea. He made it all up.

He even added the name of play-by-play radio announcer Gib Shan Lee.

"It's all a matter of marketing," Hickey said. "Everything else in the column was true. Some people thought Won Sok Hung was real. They didn't know it was a joke. We had a copy boy in the sports department who actually bet on the games with other members of the department. The other guys would give him so many points he always bet against Pusan State. He lost every week. I made sure that Pusan State covered the spread. The copy boy is now a doctor."

Won Sok Hung's exploits grew more incredible with each martini. The Pusan State Panthers crushed such Korean Big Ten rivals as the Inchon Ironmen, Taegu Terrapins, Wonson Wolverines and Pyongyang Patriots. All of these were famous datelines from the Korean War, which was still fresh in our memories.

Readers wanted to see a picture of Won Sok Hung and it took Hickey four weeks to find one in the musty files of the newspaper morgue. The half-column cut was a picture of Herman Wedemeyer, a Hawaiian running back from St. Mary's College of California. Wedemeyer was real. He went on to play pro ball with the Los Angeles Dons and Baltimore Colts in the old All-America Conference.

Game by game, Hickey led us to the Sake Bowl in Tokyo's Fujiyama Stadium on New Year's Day, which pitted Pusan State against the Fuiyon U. Flyers from the island of Hokkaido. Coached by the cunning Kato Yamamoto and led by Shugi "Crazylegs" Nakamura, Fuiyon U. had reached that final game with crushing victories over the Okinawa Owls, 44-0, and Iwo Jima Islanders, 35-0.

Hickey's account of the Sake Bowl covered an entire page in The Plain Dealer, including another blurry black-and-white picture that he discovered in the files. Pusan State won the Sake Bowl, 42-41, in a finish so bizarre it could take place only in the imagination of an Irishman sitting at a bar drinking martinis. The copy boy lost 20 bucks.

Sports editor Hal Lebovitz got a kick out of the series, which grew like an oak tree from one single acorn. Other editors, however, were not entertained.

"They cut down an entire forest to print that story of the Sake Bowl, a game that never really happened," complained one newsroom editor, "and I can't get one paragraph in the paper about a little war developing in Vietnam."

You can't say the guy didn't have a point. A sense of humor, no, but a valid point, yes.

Won Sok Hung had his season of fame and was not heard from again for many years, until Hickey expanded his tale into a book, "The Year of the Panther." Hickey personally took it to publishers in New York.

"Sports books don't sell unless they're raunchy," one editor told him.

Another editor said, "Is this supposed to be funny?"

"I snatched the manuscript back and walked out," Hickey recalled.

In the year 2000 the book was published locally and Hickey held a book signing at the Great Lakes Brewery. Between signatures he gulped down martinis, which made me think there must be a sequel coming. But no, that thought vanished when The Plain Dealer reviewed the book. It was not exactly friendly. The book editor called it the most racist book she ever read.

I thought it was funny. Politically incorrect, maybe, but not malicious. I'd like to know what Dennis Rodman thinks.

Four Live Wires

I HAVE FOUR VERY OLD pals who surprisingly are still around despite catching about a million volts on the golf course some 40 years ago, which was precisely at the mid-point of their lives.

At the insistence of their friend, Jerry Becker, I wrote about them in The Plain Dealer on July 2, 1975, which was a very slow news day. Becker, who was the bailiff for Cuyahoga County Common Pleas Judge Leo M. Spellacy, put it to me this way, "God was sitting up there and saying to Himself, 'I owe these guys one.' Zap. He got even."

At the time, Becker was lucky. He did not call in sick. He went to work at the court house and he was not part of the group huddled under the tree at Hickory Nut Golf Course when a thunderstorm came out of nowhere and a lightning bolt caught them in its crosshairs. Sadly, Becker, a beloved figure on Cleveland's West Side, died many years ago. The other four, however, are still with us. Life isn't fair.

The four live wires were Dick "Smoke" Walsh, Marty Chambers, Gerry "the Great McGoo" McGinty and Jim Lavelle, all classmates at St. Ignatius High School in the early 1950s. They remained golfing pals for many years. You may remember that Chambers and McGinty became high school basketball coaches. Lavelle was a decent football player and he became an even better card player. Walsh was nicknamed Smoke because he was one of the five fastest high school sprinters in the state. When my children were young they asked me why we called him Smoke.

"Because he ran so fast, smoke came out of his rear end," I said.

One Saturday morning at family therapy at Herb's Tavern in

Rocky River, Smoke, who was sitting at his favorite barstool, became aware that my three little boys were standing behind him, staring at the seat of his pants.

"What are you doing back there?" he asked them.

"We're waiting to see the smoke come out of your ass," they said.

Now, let's return to the incident at Hickory Nut Golf Course.

Observers say that lightning hit a tree and then jumped to an umbrella Walsh was holding. That's the last thing any of them remembers. Walsh was the most seriously injured.

"Isn't it a shame Lavelle didn't get a bigger jolt?" Walsh said.

In a more serious vein, Walsh added, "That's the way to go. Quick and painless. I never felt a thing until later. I've always been in favor of capital punishment. The guy who invented the electric chair was a humanitarian at heart."

I guess Stephen King got it all wrong in "The Green Mile."

It wasn't funny when all four of them were lying unconscious on the golf course. All golfers have their heroes, with Arnold Palmer and Jack Nicklaus leading the way for old-timers like us, but my four live wires vote for a man named Paul Gaultierre of Garfield Heights.

Gaultierre, a machine repairman at the Ford plant on Brookpark Road, was sitting in the clubhouse sipping a beer and waiting for his Ford plant league to start teeing off at 5:30 when a groundskeeper burst through the door seeking help for the stricken golfers.

"I had some medical training in the Navy in World War II and then some Red Cross training," said Gaultierre, who was 50 at the time.

First he saved the lives of Walsh and Chambers, and then administered first aid to McGinty and Lavelle. He found that Walsh and Chambers had swallowed their tongues and were slowly choking to death. Walsh's heartbeat was 14, which is only a few beats away from Holy Cross Cemetery.

"I took one look at Walsh and knew he was in trouble," said

Gaultierre. "I knew by the color of his face. It was blue. I opened his mouth and pulled his tongue out of his throat and pried it down with my comb."

There, that's proof that God exists and that he loves us. Otherwise, the first respondent would have been a bald guy.

"One of the guys I worked with in the shop for many years was an epileptic," Gaultierre continued. "Every once in a while he had a seizure. One time I had to pry his mouth open with a screwdriver to get his tongue out of his throat. It was a lot easier with Walsh and Chambers. They were relaxed."

Walsh's wife, Mary Helen, recalls getting a phone call from their family doctor, Bill Mahoney, who also happened to be chief of staff at Southwest Hospital.

"Dick's been hit by lightning," he said. "Dick is alive. I don't often get the chance to tell the wife that their husband is alive."

Luckily, they all recovered quickly, although they were still sore and still in the hospital when I wrote their story. The big reason everyone at Southwest General Hospital rejoiced at their imminent release was that they were incorrigible, ungrateful and disruptive patients.

"The first thing I remember when I regained consciousness was Chambers threatening to hit the dietician with a malpractice suit," said Walsh. "They served fish on Friday and McGinty said he saw a lone angler with his line down an open manhole on Bagley Road."

It became increasingly difficult for the staff to engender sympathy for them. One nurse said their hospital manners were shocking.

McGinty turned his hospital gown around with the open part in front and then paraded up and down the hospital corridors, terrifying patients and visitors.

Anna B. Chambers, who was married to Marty Chambers, said that the electricity burned them wherever metal touched their bodies. She said the soles of their feet were burned because of the metal cleats in their golf shoes. They were burned where medals, watches, belt buckles and zippers touched them. Zippers? "Yes, even there," said Anna B.

The coins in Walsh's pocket were melted into a solid lump. Walsh conceded that it was a learning experience.

"Keep in mind," he said, "if you're ever on the golf course when a thunderstorm hits, always let the tall guy hold the umbrella."

Soccer's Been Good to Me

I HAVE MANY FRIENDS WHO neither share nor understand my interest in soccer, and I have no problem with that. It's a world game but it's not an American game. Americans become mildly interested when our national teams play in the World Cup or Olympics but when those events are over, everyone goes back to their baseball, football and basketball.

Not me. I have a permanent soft spot in my heart for the game. To paraphrase an old comedy line, "Soccer has been very, very good to me."

In the first place, soccer was educational. When I covered amateur soccer for The Plain Dealer in the 1960s, it was an ethnic game and my first teacher was Gianfranco Borroni, who answered to Frank. He called me looking for publicity for the local adult amateur league and that was the beginning of a life-long friendship.

In those days the Italians had a team, the Germans had a couple of teams, and the Hungarians, Serbians and Croatians, of course, had teams. Everybody had an accent. Oddly, there was no team associated with the English and so Jimmy McMillan played for the Italians and worked on his accent.

Fifty years later Frank and I still appreciate the rivalry between the Serbians and the Croatians, the most intense in all of soccer. There is nothing funny about their rivalry. The poor referees who officiated games between the Serbs and the Croats feared for their lives. They deserved hazardous duty pay. One game ended with both sides chasing the referee, the first time the Serbs and Croats agreed on anything.

"Do you remember Lucky Kramer and his gun?" Frank asked.

Did I remember! I wrote about it in The Plain Dealer. Kramer, a prominent referee for decades, worked as a security guard in real life and had a license to pack a gun. On one particular Sunday he arrived to referee the Serbian-Croatian game with his gun sticking out of his waistband. He wanted everybody from both teams to see it. Lucky was no Rodney Dangerfield. He finally got respect and safe passage to his car after the game.

Well, in 1967 soccer turned pro in this country. The 1966 World Cup final, which England won 4-2 over West Germany in London's Wembley Stadium, was televised live on NBC at 10 a.m. on a Saturday morning. With no promotion and no publicity, it actually scored a measurable rating.

Monday morning when the ratings were posted in New York, a clamor went up and down Madison Avenue like a dinner bell. Professional soccer was the next big thing, said big money. Within months the first league was slapped together. Called the United Soccer Association, it launched in the spring of 1967. Such breathless haste called for a radical approach. There was no time to actually scour the world for players but big money could scour the world for teams. That's what it did. The 12 original members of the United Soccer Association imported established teams from around the world to represent them in their inaugural season. Cleveland made a deal with Stoke City of England's First Division, which now is known as the Premier League.

Owners of the Cleveland franchise were none other than Vernon Stouffer and Gabe Paul, the owners of the Indians. Neither one gave a hoot about soccer, but they felt that if a soccer team shared the Stadium and competed with them for fans and sponsorship money, it would be prudent to own the competition.

Hal Lebovitz assessed the situation thusly. He believed that the chances of this team succeeding were remote and he was correct. The Stokers lasted for only two years and lost a million dollars a year, which was more than the Indians' entire player payroll.

As sports editor of The Plain Dealer, Hal also did not want Stouffer and Paul to blame him for their failure. He had seen that

happen before. In 1946 Cleveland was an original member of the
NBA. The league was founded by arena owners in the eastern
half of the country for the purpose of providing dates to keep
their arenas busy. In those days, very few arenas or ballparks
were built by cities. They were privately owned. In the case of
the NBA, the original 11 cities were Boston, New York, Chicago,
Detroit, Philadelphia, Washington, Providence, Toronto, Pittsburgh, St. Louis and Cleveland.

The following year four teams did not return, including
Cleveland, whose owner Al Sutphin directly blamed the three
Cleveland newspapers. Not only were they non-supportive of
pro basketball, sports editor Gordon Cobbledick of The Plain
Dealer was disinterested and sports editor Whitey Lewis of the
Cleveland Press was openly hostile.

The early years of the NBA were chaotic enough. By 1949
there were 17 teams and within a year six of those were gone.
It was tough enough with newspaper support but impossible
without.

"I don't want them to point their fingers at The Plain Dealer
when they fail," Hal said to me. "We're going to cover them like
a big-league team. You're our soccer writer."

"I don't know diddley about soccer except for Frank Borroni
and a couple of Hungarians," I said.

"Well, then go to England and learn it. Spend a couple of
weeks with that Stoke City team," Hal said. "And as long as you're
over there, find an auto race to cover."

It took me about half a day to put together a schedule that
included two weeks writing about soccer in England and one
week covering the Grand Prix of Monaco in Monte Carlo.

Did I say, "Soccer was very, very good to me?"

The Stoke City team treated me like royalty. One day I was the
guest of team president G. W. Taylor for horse racing at Epsom
Downs. We rode together in the back seat of his chauffeured
Rolls-Royce. On the way he relieved himself through a funnel,
which led to a tube that ran through a hole in the floor and
emptied on the road. Wow.

Mr. Taylor owned race horses and had one running in the first race. I was obligated to bet on him, and he finished out of the money. In the third race I bet on a filly named Shamrock's Beauty, who pitched her jockey at the clubhouse turn and romped home riderless and happy. (No, I did not hide my losses on my expense account.)

I rode the train to London with Stoke City to a game at Chelsea. I honed my taste for ox tail soup at bars and restaurants and shared countless hours at pubs with players who would be my companions for much of the summer.

I sat with a retiring player, Dennis Viollet, while he sold tickets to his own retirement game. Because the pension plan was so poor in those days, star players were honored with testimonial games, a type of all-star game, with all the revenue going to the player.

Dennis told me stories that American sportswriters rarely hear or write about. He grew up in Manchester during World War II and remembered the siege when German bombers targeted his city for four straight days.

"I can recall the sky at night being solid crimson from the flames. I can remember awakening at all hours of the night to go into the basement," Viollet said. "My mother wanted to send me to the country to live with my aunt and uncle until the siege was over. I refused to go. Then I was watching a German plane being chased across the sky by two Spitfires. He dropped his bombs, to get more speed I guess. They landed on my aunt and uncle's farm."

When he was 25 years old, he survived the horrible 1958 Manchester United plane crash in Munich, a tragedy which took 23 lives, including eight Manchester United players. They were returning on a chartered British European Airways flight from an international match in Belgrade and had stopped to refuel in Munich. A 3-3 tie with the Red Star team had put Manchester United in the semifinals of the European Cup based on aggregate goals in two games.

Dennis was hospitalized with head injuries and was unable to play as Manchester United's remaining players lost to AC Milan on aggregate goals, 5-2. Real Madrid went on to win the European Cup championship over AC Milan.

"I thought about it for a long time. I lost a lot of close friends. I still don't talk about it much," he said to me.

I filed stories almost every day. Thank God that The Plain Dealer was the largest paper in Ohio because my phone bills alone would have crippled a smaller paper.

Then it was off to Monaco for the Grand Prix through the city streets of Monte Carlo, a race won by New Zealander Denis Hulme, his first ever Formula I victory. Denis was at the top of his game, but he was overshadowed by other events.

The night before the race I sucked down French beers in the first-floor bar of the Hotel de Paris, smack on the square across from the Casino. And, like everybody else in the crowded lounge, I stared the entire night at a tiny cocktail table in the middle of the room where Elizabeth Taylor, Richard Burton and Graham Hill were pounding them down. Every time Graham Hill reached for a cigarette, Elizabeth Taylor grabbed Richard Burton's golden lighter and lit it. This was 1967 and Elizabeth was at the absolute top of her game.

Graham Hill stayed up too late, but the next day he still managed to slip into second place with 10 laps to go and share the podium with Hulme and the Royal Family. The Prince and Princess of Monaco and their three children presented the silver cup to the winner, but runner-up Graham Hill wasn't complaining. There he was with Princess Grace, who in 1967 was still the most beautiful princess in the world. Not a bad weekend for Graham. You'd think he was Cary Grant, rubbing elbows with both Elizabeth Taylor and Grace Kelly within 24 hours.

But nobody was smiling. As with so many races in those days, it was a tearfully sad Sunday in Monaco. Lorenzo Bandini, 29 years old, the star of the Ferrari team, was killed in a fiery crash while running in second place with only 10 laps to go. He crashed into a light pole on the tiled promenade overlooking the harbor and his car immediately caught fire. He was burned over 70 percent of his body. After several agonizing hours in the hospital, Bandini passed away. When told he had died, his pregnant wife fainted.

I flew home and soon was joined by the Stoke City team. We gallivanted back and forth across the country, playing in front of crowds averaging 5,000 in huge American stadiums. Soccer was going nowhere. Hal was right. Nobody could blame The Plain Dealer. In the middle of July, I stopped in Pat Joyce's Tavern on East Sixth Street and bartender Walter Kulon said, "Are you still writing for the paper?"

"Of course, I am. I'm covering soccer," I said.

"That explains it," said Kulon. "I haven't read anything you've written all summer."

During the subsequent winter, Gabe Paul and Vernon Stouffer, assured that soccer was no threat to them, persuaded Ted Bonda and Howard Metzenbaum to take over the team. In year one of the great soccer experiment, Paul and Stouffer lost a million dollars. In year two, Bonda and Metzenbaum lost another million dollars and canceled the experiment.

Over the next four decades several low-budget professional teams came and went, usually playing at Finney Stadium in Berea. When Randy Lerner was a student at Shaker Heights High School he developed an interest in soccer while working as a ball boy for one of those teams, gathering balls and picking up socks and jocks after practice. Lerner, who inherited the Cleveland Browns upon the death of his father, later bought the Aston Villa soccer team in England's Premier League. He said the soccer team enjoyed a place in his heart. The Browns were only part of his family's holdings.

As Walter Kulon said, "That explains it."

Grin and Bear It

TUCKER KEEGAN, A LONG-RETIRED advertising salesman for The Plain Dealer, has crammed an inordinate amount of living into his 70 years. He never missed a party and danced every dance. His life has been one continuous Beer Barrel Polka. In fact, it is remarkable that he is still living at all. Too many weekends at Put-In-Bay in the company of Pat Dailey have taken their toll.

In the twilight of his years, however, he seems to be haunted by one major regret. He never beat the famous wrestling bear at the Sportsmen's Show.

The Sportsmen's Show at the downtown Public Hall was one of Cleveland's mid-winter highlights. As kids we rode the No. 25 Madison trolley to Public Square and then walked a couple of blocks to the Public Hall, where we marveled at the acres of hunting gear, fishing gear and camping gear. I had no intention of actually using any of that stuff, but it was fun to fantasize about living in the woods.

For many years, staples of the Sportsmen's Show were the live lectures and presentations by such legendary outdoorsmen as Joe "Castaway" Kulis, who pioneered hunting and fishing shows on local Cleveland television and radio. He was there to see the Sportsmen's Show begin a downward spiral when it moved from Public Hall to the I-X Center and shrunk from 10 days to four.

"The show at Public Hall was a thousand percent better than the I-X Center," said Kulis, who appeared at 45 straight Sportsmen's Shows. "There were a lot of reasons. The Public Hall had a wooden floor and a big stage. It had a real orchestra. It had actual shows with interesting acts. They had the wrestling bear, for example. They said the bear was put on his back only twice.

Once was by a high school or college wrestler who got him quick, caught him by surprise. I don't remember the second one."

Tucker Keegan appeared on the stage once, which became his personal highlight and his biggest disappointment.

In 1977 Keegan and his Plain Dealer advertising colleague Mike Chirdon were selected from among dozens of entries to grapple Victor, the 650-pound Alaskan brown bear, on the main stage at the Sportsmen's Show.

"We had calls from more than 200 people who wanted to wrestle Victor," said Joe Madigan, the show's public relations man.

"We were lucky to be picked," said Chirdon.

"I'm not so sure," said Madigan. "Victor's been in a surly mood all day. His trainer says he never saw him that mean."

"We could come back tomorrow," said Keegan.

"Not on your life," said Madigan. "You get this chance only once. There is no tomorrow."

Chirdon was realistic. "I'm not going out there to be a hero, just to actualize a fantasy," he said.

Madigan also was Victor's booking agent. He was always on the lookout for celebrity opponents, such as big, hairy pro football players. Between shows Victor's trainer, George Allen, known as Gorgeous George, met the future Hall of Fame fullback Larry Csonka at Pat Joyce's restaurant across the street. Gorgeous George attempted to persuade Csonka to wrestle Victor. Csonka's agent Ed Keating almost had a heart attack when he heard about it. Keating advised Csonka to get as far away from the bear as he could.

"Too bad," said Gorgeous George. "Victor would have had no trouble with Csonka." The trainer claimed that Victor already owned decisions over three Browns football linemen—Walter Johnson, Dick Schafrath and Lyle Alzado—in addition to the monstrous Ernie Ladd.

The bear act was at the end of an hour-long stage show. As Chirdon and Keegan waited nervously, strangers sidled up to them conspiratorially with words of caution. Even Gorgeous George commented about the bear's ill humor.

"They wouldn't let us do this if we could actually get hurt, would they?" Chirdon rationalized.

"You signed the liability release, didn't you?" said Gorgeous George.

"A guy told us to stay away from his muzzle," Chirdon said to the trainer.

"That's right," said George.

"And he told us to stay away from his front paws," said Chirdon.

"That's right," said George.

"He said to stay away from the back paws, too," said Chirdon.

"That's right," said George.

"What does that leave us?" Keegan asked, his voice quivering in panic.

"Not much," said George. "One other thing. Don't pull his ears or gouge his eyes. If you do, I'll walk off the stage and leave you alone with him. I won't be responsible for what happens."

Ann Strobel, who was the show's fly-casting expert, had seen the bear's show many times. Since I was present to document the event and ensure that everyone got a fair fight, Strobel confided to me.

"They have nothing to worry about. All Victor does is love you to death," Ann said.

I kept this information to myself.

Chirdon went first and he had his moments. Staying low to the mat, spinning and diving, Chirdon squirmed in and out of the bear's declawed grasp. Chirdon reached a hind foot and tugged. Victor toppled over on his back. Bringing Victor down was a rarity. This may have been the second takedown Castaway Kulis mentioned. Chirdon brought down Victor a second time, which angered the bear, and Chirdon's night was over.

"I don't remember much. Every time I looked up, he was there," said Chirdon. "It seemed like 20 minutes, but I know it probably was less than a minute. The next time I hear a story about a man chasing away a bear with a knife or a stick, it's all malarkey. The bear was never in any trouble."

Keegan followed Chirdon to the mat and spent most of his time on his back, while the bear hovered over him, salivating on his face.

"Victor made this rumbling sound from deep in his body. He smacked me around pretty good," said Keegan.

To this day Keegan believes Victor intentionally took a dive for Chirdon.

"I told Mike that the trainer had hand signals with the bear. How else would he get the bear off him? I think they used Mike as a ringer to get more people to wrestle the bear, by showing that it was possible to get the bear on his back. Mike didn't believe me. He thinks he really did it," said Keegan.

In the meantime, Keegan hungered for a second chance with the bear. Most people are content to say, "Yes, I wrestled a bear," and then move on. Not Keegan. A few weeks later he got his second chance. Victor was appearing at an East Side mall, taking on anybody willing to pay 10 bucks. Keegan slipped away from work in the middle of the day for another shot at immortality. Once again, it was not a good idea.

Keegan looked like a guy on a trampoline. Down he went. Up he bounced. Down he went. Up he bounced. Down he went and this time Keegan stayed down. Frankly, that was the best thing that could have happened to him.

If he had won, whom could he tell? He was supposed to be calling on customers 20 miles away. The temptation to tell the world would have been irresistible. Keegan was never any good at fighting off temptation.

The Eagles Have Landed

THE FAMILY OF BALD eagles who set up housekeeping in a tree looking down on an Avon Lake school yard back in 2014 must have been looking for a home close to schools in a nice suburb. Here in northeastern Ohio most eagles build their nests far away from people, in solitary areas along the Lake Erie shoreline and the rivers that feed it.

But here was a feathered family that settled smack in the middle of a populous suburb. Children were admonished to tone down the noise in the playground. Neighborhood residents respected the new family's need for quiet and privacy. They watched. They took pictures. They kept notebooks. All from a distance. They never interfered with the eagles.

From his front yard directly across the street at the corner of Redwood and Parkwood Avenues, Terry Wyrock studied the pair from the first day they started building their nest. He took photographs with a special lens that enlarged the pictures tenfold, documenting the daily progress. Later he added a telescope pointed directly at their nest. Terry was a veritable peeping tom.

"The female selected the location," Terry Wyrock said. "Just like human families. The female selected the tree and the branch. She picked up the first stick and actually presented it to the male. It was as though she told him, build it here, about 40 feet high."

Wyrock said that the male sometimes placed a stick incorrectly, at least not according to her plan. To get his attention she bit him on the shoulder. Their dynamics were almost human.

Wyrock discovered that the eagles spent most of their time away from their nest, hunting and fishing. The Lake Erie shoreline is about a mile away.

Shortly after the nest was finished she laid two eggs. One eaglet survived and soon was airborne. The second year, another eaglet survived. The family is growing. Wyrock has sharp pictures of the male eagle feeding fish to one of the youngsters.

Ron Jantz, a media professor at Lorain County Community College, lives nearby and is working on a television documentary about the eagles.

A century ago farmers eliminated the deer in Ohio to protect their crops. They poisoned and shot every last deer. They also eliminated wolves, cougars and bears to protect their livestock. In the 1920s hunters lobbied the state legislature to bring back the deer for hunting, and they got their wish. Beware of what you wish for. We are now overrun by almost one million deer. They forgot to bring back the wolves, cougars and bears.

There was a time when eagles were virtually extinct in Ohio because of DDT that the farmers used on their crops. The unintended consequence of DDT was that it got into everything eagles ate and drank and rendered their eggshells too thin to survive. In the 1970s DDT was outlawed and the eagles got a second chance. Their eggshells are strong and thick again.

Without DDT the farmers turned to other fertilizers which are poisoning Lake Erie. At times the water around Toledo is not potable. In the summer of 2014 one of my son's in-laws had a family reunion in Toledo. Everyone was asked to bring a case of bottled water.

God had a pretty good plan when He put it all together and we've done nothing but screw it up.

That leads me to Canada geese. It's illegal to kill them, we can't send them back and we can't control their poop. I wish someone would explain that to me.

The Body at Clifton Beach

WHEN THE BODY WASHED up at Clifton Beach in the summer of 1959, it was my lucky day. An immigrant from eastern Europe had slipped off the rocks while fishing near East 55th Street and wasn't seen for 30 days. The unpredictable tides of Lake Erie slowly took him to the mouth of the Rocky River, 10 miles to the west, where he popped up near the sandy shore of the private beach in Lakewood.

Sue Westerkamp was the lifeguard. She squinted into the afternoon sun and wondered if that was a body floating toward her. Her younger sister, Sally, and my sister, Cathy, both in the eighth grade, swam out to investigate and, true enough, it was a body. Sally reached out and touched the arm, which came off in her hand. Sally and Cathy were killing a warm afternoon at the beach, which they usually did, and they never expected they would wind up on a coroner's report.

After a certain amount of shrieking, they managed to bring the body ashore—what was left of it, anyway. They then scurried to the only phone at Clifton Beach, a pay phone near the guard's shack, and they made their first important call. Cathy called home and I answered the phone. She explained what happened and I reassured her. "I'll take care of everything," I said.

Everyone settled down. I was, after all, the older brother. I was in college.

Was my first phone call to the police or the fire department? It was to neither. My first call was to radio station WERE, the flagship station of the Indians radio network. WERE was offering two box seats to an Indians game for the best news tip of the week and I figured that poor devil's death made me a winner.

After the radio newsman had taken down my name and address, I told him, "Wait 60 seconds before you call the Lakewood police. They're my next call."

A week later two box-seat tickets arrived in the mail, proving the theory that when somebody has bad luck, somebody else gets an equal amount of good luck. It's how the world stays in balance. I learned that from "Seinfeld" years later.

I wanted to share my good fortune with my close friend Jerry McKenna, who had just left the seminary at Notre Dame after three years and was trying to catch up as a regular student by taking summer courses at Western Reserve University on the East Side. Jerry had no money and was living for the summer at the Newman Club, which was sort of a Catholic fraternity without the beer and pizza.

He was excited about the game. Jerry was a football man, but you had to be pumped up about box seats because these were not ordinary box seats that anyone could buy at the ticket window. They were directly from the Indians' flagship radio station. A man died for those tickets. Furthermore, the Indians were in a torrid pennant race with the Chicago White Sox. The Indians fell short. They finished second to the White Sox with the Yankees in third place, but that is incidental to the main story.

Jerry and I agreed to meet before the game at about 7 o'clock at Moriarty's bar on East Sixth Street. It's still there, by the way. Same place, same name. Jerry had no car. He would be taking a bus downtown but he knew where the bar was.

It turned out that Jerry ran into a conflict that night. He could not get away. He couldn't call me because he forgot the name of the bar. He knew how to get there, but with no name he couldn't look it up in the phone book. I sat there inning after inning, listening to the game on the radio. Jimmy Dudley and Bob Neal, two guys who hated each other, were the announcers on the little radio behind the bar at Moriarty's.

I'm fairly bright. By the time the game ended I realized Jerry wasn't coming. I tossed my last 50 cents on the bar for the bartender and stumbled out into the night, full of beer but with empty pockets.

I was barely out the door and on the sidewalk when a panhandler approached me and begged for 50 cents so he could get a bed in a flophouse for the night. Just then I heard a roll of thunder overhead. Damn, I thought, I just left my last 50 cents on the bar. I really felt bad about that. You could smell rain in the air and this poor guy had no roof over his head. He was an old-timer with a weathered face and gray hair.

"Come with me," I said to him. "I'll bring you home with me."

I brought him home, fixed him a couple of cheeseburgers which he wolfed down as though he hadn't eaten in a week, and sent him to bed in my room, in my bed. I slept on a back porch. That night it rained like a monsoon.

In the morning the family started getting up. My mother and father, my grandmother and my two sisters. A lot of women in that house.

"Where's Dan?" somebody asked.

"He seems to be asleep on the back porch," someone said.

"Who's that in his bed?" they all wondered.

All the women huddled around my bedroom door, puzzled by the wheezing. The old boy seemed to have a wheezing condition when he slept. Some guys snore. This guy wheezed.

To this day my sister Ruth claims she thought I had brought home one of my pals. She fixed her hair real nice to meet the overnight guest.

Finally, they slowly opened the door and to their horror discovered this street person, old and not too clean, wheezing away in my bed. Once again, earth's balance was in play. It was my bad luck that the tickets went to waste. It was the old timer's good luck that he got a meal and a dry bed.

Nobody made a federal case about it then. My mother fixed him breakfast and my father, on his way to work, delivered him back downtown.

Not long ago my sister, Ruth, and I were reminiscing about that night.

"Oh, Mom was so mad at you," Ruth said.

"I didn't realize that," I said. "She said nothing to me."

"You were lucky," Ruth said.

Albert Belle: Bad Attitude

WHEN ALBERT BELLE WAS called up to the Indians for the first time in 1989, he knew nobody. He had no friends. When he left town as a free agent after the 1996 season, nothing had changed. He still had no friends.

During Albert's glory days here, Malley's Candy, one of Cleveland's most revered companies, honored him with a chocolate bar. There was a little press conference at Jacobs Field to announce their relationship. Bill and Adele Malley, who headed the family company, were at the podium passing out "Albert Belle Bars." The newspaper and television reporters were there. Everybody was there except Albert.

"He told me when he left the park last night that he wouldn't be there," one of the clubhouse workers said to me.

He didn't forget. He didn't oversleep. He didn't care. I was outraged. The Malleys were friends of mine and he insulted them. I couldn't get to my computer fast enough to rip him open from head to feet in my column the next day.

Before the next day's game I was hanging out in the Indians' dugout when Albert walked by. He looked at me and sneered. "Nice article," he said contemptuously.

Indians' first-base coach Dave Nelson, an old friend of mine going back to the 1960s, came up.

"Albert's a friend of mine," said Dave. "I'm really sorry you wrote that."

When Albert returned to Cleveland the next year as a member of the Chicago White Sox, Nelson approached his old "friend" with his arms spread wide to give him a hug. Albert turned his back and walked away.

"You never know which Albert is going to show up," Nelson said once.

I knew which Albert would show up—the angry, selfish one. Look at his history.

While playing college baseball for LSU in 1987, he went into the stands after a fan at Mississippi State who taunted him by calling him "Buckwheat." I'll give Albert a pass on that one.

In 1990 he spent 10 weeks in the Cleveland Clinic for alcohol problems and anger management after he destroyed a sink in the Colorado Springs clubhouse during a post-game tirade. That is when he changed his first name from Joey to Albert.

Temper tantrums cut short his 1990 Puerto Rican winter-league season. Evidently rehab and anger management in the Cleveland Clinic didn't work.

On May 11, 1991, a heckler in the left-field seats caught Albert's ear with shouts of "Hey, Joey! Keg Party!" Albert tried to ignore him until the heckler—a fellow named Jeff Pillar—yelled, "Throw me a ball." That was Pillar's big mistake. A foul ball had just been hit down the left-field line by Ron Tingley of the California Angels. Albert reached down, picked it up, and drilled a fastball directly into Pillar's chest. Pillar was treated in the Indians' first aid room and then he went directly to Channel 8, where I was the Saturday sports anchor, to show me the indentation the ball made in the middle of his chest. I sympathized with him and asked him to keep me informed about his lawsuit. Albert was suspended six games for that.

In 1993 he had a dustup in a Cleveland billiards parlor with a guy named William Kelley who repeatedly called him "Joey." Albert was sensitive about his former name.

Cork spilled all over the infield in Comiskey Park in 1994 when Albert's bat shattered. He was suspended for seven games. Albert claimed the White Sox stole his bat and corked it. He should have been suspended for seven more games for telling such an outrageous story.

During the 1995 World Series he went berserk against television broadcaster Hannah Storm as she conducted pre-game interviews in the Indians' dugout. Albert was fined $50,000 for his obscenity-laced explosion.

On Halloween night of 1995 Albert jumped in his Jeep and chased five teenagers because they threw eggs at his house. I'm giving Albert a pass on that one, too. The police report, which never was made public, revealed the kids climbed over the wall of Albert's gated community and had been tormenting him and his father much of the night.

The low point in Albert's career occurred on April 6, 1996, a frigid day in Cleveland early in his final season with the Indians.

Tony Tomsic, a photographer for Sports Illustrated magazine, was taking pictures of Albert for a cover story. When he focused on Albert during pre-game calisthenics, Albert, for whatever strange reasons, did not want his picture taken.

He was the cover story in a national publication, for Pete's sake!

Albert wagged his finger at Tomsic to stop. "No, no, no," said Albert. Tomsic is not a confrontational guy, so he backed off.

But a few minutes later Tomsic noticed Albert loitering in short center field playing long toss with Manny Ramirez. Tomsic was on the track near third base and he had Albert right in the middle of his viewfinder. Click. Click. Click.

"I heard some yelling from the players and then I heard a ball hit behind me in the seats. I don't know whether it went over my head, next to me or what. Did you ever hear a baseball crash into the plastic seats of a stadium? It sounds like a gunshot," Tomsic recalled earlier this year.

Tomsic would know about gunshots. He covered the race riots here when he worked for the Cleveland Press earlier in his career. Tomsic was still shooting, but in his peripheral vision he saw something coming for his head.

"I instinctively put up my hand to protect my face and Albert's next throw hit me on my hand, on my knuckles," said Tomsic, who remembers the next exchange vividly.

"I told you not to get my picture, asshole," Albert shouted.

"Would you repeat that?" Tomsic yelled back.

Albert said it again, verbatim.

Many of Albert's teammates were stunned. Tomsic was a bloody mess. His knuckles were cut. One of the trainers took him in, cleaned up his hand and put a bandage on it.

"I'd like to forget the whole thing," he said at the time. "I feel bad for the club. I don't want to cause trouble for them. If he had hit me in the face with the ball, I would really have been upset."

Tomsic, who grew up in Cleveland Heights, came from the old school that said you fought your own battles.

For two weeks nothing happened, but the baseball writers wouldn't let it die. Most of them hated Belle, for good reason. Belle's miserable disposition had taken the glow off the Indians' World Series season the year before. Many of Belle's teammates also hated him or were afraid of him.

"Don't get involved with him," cautioned utility infielder Alvaro Espinoza. "He's crazy."

Newspapers all over the country picked up the story. The Washington Post published a Sunday editorial. The Boston Globe went heavy on it. USA Today covered it almost daily. The Cleveland and Akron papers sounded off. When Phyllis Merhige, the American League's public relations vice-president, came to Cleveland to "collect information," she also collected a crowd. Merhige introduced Tomsic to another PR person this way: "This is the guy who caused all the trouble."

Who knows what that meant?

In the meantime, Belle was telling preposterous lies when officials from the Indians and the league interviewed him about the incident. For one, he said it was an accident while he was playing long toss with Manny Ramirez.

Finally, Tomsic caved in and sued Albert. His lawyer was a former Clevelander, Fred Weisman, who knew his way around baseball. The suit languished in Common Pleas Court during the winter. One judge retired before it could land on his docket. Another judge, a woman, wanted no part of it.

The following March, Tomsic was in spring training when Indians pitcher Orel Hershiser waved him over.

"How come nobody's taken my deposition?" said Hershiser.

"What?" Tomsic responded.

"Yeah, I was standing right next to Belle when he threw at you. I told him to go right over to you and apologize. He refused to do that," said Hershiser.

"Why do you want to get involved?" said Tomsic.

"Because it's the right thing to do," said Hershiser.

That was the key testimony. Belle's lawyers advised him to settle before the case went to trial and he did.

Tomsic, who is almost 80 years old and in retirement lives in Westlake, cashed a nice check but to this day refuses to say how much he collected, which is typical in this kind of settlement. One thing the settlement did not include was an apology. Tomsic and Belle have not spoken in almost 20 years.

My last memory of the great slugger was in a barren Indians locker room in January 1997. It was the middle of winter. All the lockers had been cleaned out. In front of Belle's old locker, however, was a large cardboard shipping box, about the size of a washing machine. It was overflowing with mail and packages, love letters from his fans.

"What's gonna happen to Albert's mail?" I asked one of the clubhouse workers.

"It will be thrown out. Albert doesn't want any of it," said the clubbie.

From a safe distance, the kids adored him. That's the danger in getting too close. The awe and wonder don't travel well.

1. I rode my thumb across the country in the 1950s and early '60s. Here I am hitchhiking back to Fort Hood, Texas, in 1962. Long distance truckers always picked up soldiers. *(author's collection)*

2. Dick Zunt and I were the two best-dressed characters on the high school beat at The Plain Dealer early in our careers. We never worried about forgetting to zip up our zippers. With sport coats like these, who would notice? (*author's collection*)

3. Owner Vlado "Wally" Pisorn poses in front of his Harbor Inn saloon in September 2015. Now in his 70s he is tired and planning to sell the bar and retire. (*Chuck Murr*)

4. Cavs owner Ted Stepien rejoices after throwing softball from perch near top of Terminal Tower. On successive throws he hit a car, a man and a woman. No one died. *(Cleveland Press Collection, Cleveland State University Archives)*

5. Legendary boxing promoter Don King is surrounded by his oldest advisors (plus an old boxing writer) at Cleveland City Hall in February 2015. From left, lawyer George Forbes, Don King, author Dan Coughlin, and lawyer Clarence Rogers. Don wisely surrounded himself with lawyers. *(Paul Sciria)*

6. David Dwoskin, the man who put Stadium Mustard in your neighborhood grocery store in 1969, proudly displays his beloved mustard. *(David Dwoskin)*

7. Jim Mueller, seen here with heavyweight champion Larry Holmes, humbled Howard Cosell on January 23, 1973, in Kingston, Jamaica, when George Foreman took the heavyweight crown from Joe Frazier. *(courtesy of Jim Mueller)*

8. Jake LaMotta punished dozens of opponents in the 1950s. The movie "Raging Bull" documented LaMotta's brutality. Check out the noses on both these guys. *(author's collection)*

9. Lee Walczuk, all-scholastic basketball player from St. Edward, receiving one of his many awards at the Cleveland Press banquet in 1966. *(Cleveland Press Collection, Cleveland State University Archives)*

10. Phil Argento of West High, who scored 66 points in one game, is the icon of West Senate basketball in the 1960s. He later coached at Avon Lake, Lutheran West and Lakewood high schools. *(Cleveland Press Collection, Cleveland State University Archives)*

11. Quarterback Joe Pickens leads St. Ignatius to a 34-28 victory over Cincinnati Moeller in the 1989 state championship game at Ohio Stadium in Columbus. It was the Wildcats' second straight title. Four of his grade school classmates from St. Thomas More grade school followed Joe to Ignatius and also started on the championship teams. *(St. Ignatius High School)*

12. Four old pals were lit up by a lightning bolt on a golf course in June 1975. Forty years later, in September 2015, they got together for a team picture. From left are Gerry McGinty, Jim Lavelle, Dick "Smoke" Walsh and Marty Chambers. Miraculously, they recovered and went on to live normal lives. *(Joseph F. Smith)*

13. In 1961 future tennis star Arthur Ashe and I lived in Lynchburg, Virginia, but we never met. I was a beginning sportswriter on my first job. Ashe was a middle school student. My newspaper did not cover African-American sports. Tennis public relations man Jim Passant (left) got us together at a Cleveland tournament in the early 1970s. *(Jim Passant Public Relations)*

14. Fullback Marion Motley. When the All-America Football Conference was founded in 1946, rival owners objected to African-American players, specifically Motley and Bill Willis of the Browns. Mickey McBride, who owned the Browns, scoffed in the owners' faces. *(Cleveland Press Collection, Cleveland State University Archives)*

15. That's Princess Grace of Monaco in sunglasses and white bonnet, along with her husband Prince Rainier and two of her children, at the trophy presentation following the 1967 Monaco Grand Prix. *(author's collection)*

16. Victor the Wrestling Bear is on top and Tucker Keegan is struggling underneath for the amusement of those attending the Sportsman's Show at Public Hall in the 1970s. *(author's collection*

17. Young Indians slugger Tony Horton swings for the fences and hits his third home run of the game on May 24, 1970. The Indians wore pin-striped home uniforms that season. Later that season he attempted suicide and retired permanently from baseball. *(Cleveland Press Collection, Cleveland State University Archives)*

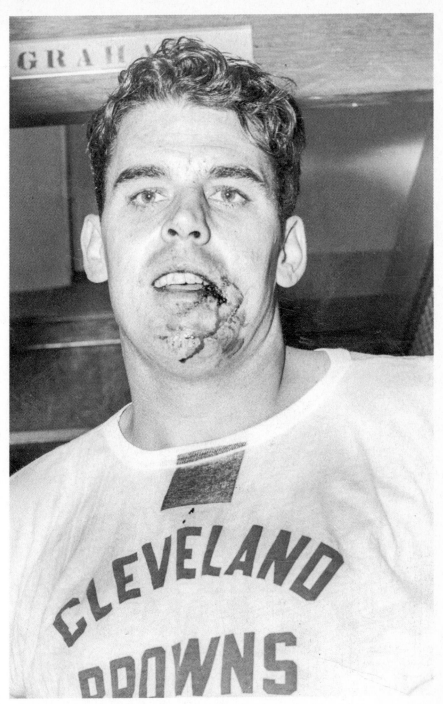

18. Browns quarterback Otto Graham with 15 stitches in his chin thanks to San Francisco 49ers defensive end Art Michalik late in the 1953 season. Graham's injury inspired development of the face mask. He was named the NFL's most valuable player that season. (*Cleveland Press Collection, Cleveland State University Archives*)

19. The great running author Jim Fixx stopped in Cleveland on his national book tour shortly before he died. *(Cleveland Press Collection, Cleveland State University Archives)*

20. Defensive lineman Bob Gain, one of the greatest who played for the Browns, lived an adventurous life. He stood up to Bear Bryant in college, flew a bombing run in Korea and survived a gunshot wound. *(Cleveland Public Library)*

21. The Browns' first coach, Paul Brown, on the practice field at Bowling Green with linebacker Lou Saban, who also went on to become a head coach in college and in pro football. The Browns conducted training camp at Bowling Green from 1946 through 1951. Later camps were at Hiram College, Kent State, Lakeland Community College and Berea. *(Cleveland Press Collection, Cleveland State University Archives)*

22. Sportscaster Nev Chandler, who had the gift of mimicry, acknowledges applause after regaling a luncheon crowd. *(author's collection)*

23. James "Mudcat" Grant began his major league baseball career with the Indians, was traded to Minnesota where he became the first African-American pitcher to win 20 games in the American League, and eventually returned to Cleveland to become a legendary Indians television announcer. Mudcat and his broadcasting partner Harry Jones were fired after the 1977 season by new WJW-TV general manager Bill Flynn, who never saw them broadcast a game. *(Cleveland Press Collection, Cleveland State University Archives)*

24. The GMC Motor Home that triggered the entire fiasco that had me locked behind bars at the Euclid Police Station in 1981. *(author's collection)*

25. The brilliant tennis promoter Bob Malaga suddenly realizes he can squeeze more people into the Harold T. Clark Stadium for the Chris Evert-Yvonne Goolagong match by re-numbering the seats. *(Cleveland Press Collection, Cleveland State University Archives)*

26. Dan Coughlin seems to be saying "Thank you" to thousands of people at the Woollybear Festival who contributed to his bank of memories which resulted in three nostalgic books. (*Bill Martin*)

1954 Revisited

IF BASEBALL COMMISSIONER FORD Frick had been as crazy in the 1950s as Commissioner Bud Selig was in the 2000s, the Indians would have won the World Series in 1954.

All we needed was to reverse the home-field advantage—start the World Series in Cleveland and not New York—and we would have won.

Since 2003, the league that wins the All-Star Game gets home-field advantage in the World Series. It's crazy. Everybody knows that. That wacky policy was adopted on the theory that it will increase interest in the All-Star Game, which is a dinosaur. There was a time, many years ago, when the All-Star Game was the one opportunity to compare the best players from the opposing leagues. No longer. That was before television and interleague play and free agency that permits players to bounce back and forth from one league to the other whenever a better deal presents itself. Nevertheless, the All-Star Game and the World Series are still connected.

If that had been the policy under Commissioner Ford Frick in 1954, Cleveland baseball would have been changed. Cleveland hosted the 1954 All-Star Game which the American League won, 11-9, on two homers by Al Rosen and one by Larry Doby. My dad and I, by the way, were among the 68,751 at the Stadium that July 13, 1954. We both wore our good suits to the game because people dressed up when they went downtown in those days. I was ghastly hot in my gray flannel suit but I thought nothing of it. I was in high school and did not have many opportunities to wear that fine suit. We took the Rapid Transit train downtown from Lakewood and walked down West Third Street to the Stadium. It was hot and sunny. There was plenty of sweat to go around. I'm sure I smelled like a locker room when we got home.

It was a spectacular summer. The Indians won 111 games, an American League record, and finished eight games ahead of the hated Yankees. We had finished second to the Yankees the previous three years so when we clinched the pennant, the Cleveland newspapers led the cheering with massive headlines. The Cleveland News hauled out war type that hadn't been used since Japan surrendered in 1945. So in October we sailed into the World Series against the New York Giants, beginning with the first two games at the Polo Grounds, the Giants' home field in Manhattan.

As for the New York Giants: Let's clear that up. We're talking about the baseball Giants. Four years later they were playing in a minor-league park in San Francisco. You know them now as the San Francisco Giants. The New York Giants are a football team that plays in New Jersey. Neither the football Giants nor New Jersey have anything to do with the 1954 World Series. As for the Cleveland News, it was an afternoon paper that went out of business in 1960. As for Japan, it is an island country in the Far East that makes automobiles.

Now you're up to date.

The Indians were heavy favorites over the Giants because they had one of the greatest pitching staffs ever assembled. The staff combined to lead the league in earned-run average and had 77 complete games. Bob Lemon and Early Wynn tied for the league lead with 23 victories. Coincidentally, Lemon and Wynn also had identical earned-run averages of 2.72. Mike Garcia led the league in earned-run average with 2.64. Three of those Indians pitchers are in the Hall of Fame—Bob Feller, Lemon and Wynn. A fourth, Hal Newhouser, ended his career as a relief pitcher with the Indians in 1954 after a long Hall of Fame career as a starter with the Detroit Tigers.

The Indians didn't have the offensive firepower of some

National League teams, but Tribe center fielder Larry Doby led the American League with 32 home runs and second baseman Roberto Avila won the batting crown at .341.

Championships, however, are not won on statistics alone. The Giants swept the Indians in four straight games, not because they were the better team, but because the Polo Grounds had the strangest dimensions in baseball.

Polo Grounds. What a name for a ballpark! They actually did play polo there from 1876 to 1889, but it was twice torn down and rebuilt and by 1954 the only horses seen there were police horses. The Polo Grounds was a fine location for anything except baseball. Some people said it was shaped like a bathtub. To me it looked like a hangar for a Goodyear blimp. Many soccer games were played there. Some famous fights, also, such as Dempsey-Firpo, the first Louis-Conn and the Patterson-Johansson rematch. The football Giants hosted NFL championship games there in 1934, '38, '44 and '46. It was in the Polo Grounds that the great sportswriter Grantland Rice composed the classic line, "Outlined against a blue gray October sky, the Four Horsemen rode again," after covering the Notre Dame-Army football game in 1924.

In 1936 the Boston Redskins played one game in the Polo Grounds en route to moving the franchise to Washington, D.C., where they remain.

The deepest part of center field looked like a tunnel. At its deepest it was 483 feet from home plate, an absurd distance. It was said that only Babe Ruth could hit a ball that far. At the other extreme, the right-field foul pole was located 258 feet from the plate, also an absurd distance.

The Series opener matched a pair of right-handers, Bob Lemon for the Indians against Sal Maglie. The Indians jumped on top, 2-0, in the first inning when Maglie hit leadoff batter Al Smith in the back and Avila followed with a single. Vic Wertz, who had been picked up early in the season in a trade with Baltimore, followed with a triple to left-center that bounced off the wall. Smith and Avila scored and the Cleveland juggernaut appeared to be on its way.

Lemon struggled early in the game. He allowed two runs in the third but that was all until the 10th, when all hell broke loose. It never should have gotten to the 10th, however.

In the top of the eighth Doby walked and Rosen beat out a single to deep shortstop. With two runners on base, Wertz stepped to the plate. Giants manager Leo Durocher was jumpy. Having seen enough of Maglie, he went to his bullpen for left-hander Don Liddle to face the left-handed hitting Wertz, who had followed his earlier triple with two singles. Wertz would go on to enjoy one of the more memorable World Series in baseball history. He wound up going 8 for 16.

Wertz had enjoyed fine seasons in Detroit early in his career, but by 1954 he was collecting too many stickers on his suitcase. He was with Baltimore when the Indians acquired him in a trade to remedy a mistake. The Indians desperately needed a first baseman. They had switched Rosen from third base to first base to make room in the lineup for spring-training sensation Rudy Regalado. Known as Rudy the Red Hot Rapper, Regalado opened the season at third base and immediately cooled off. Rosen went to first base and promptly broke his finger learning an unfamiliar position. Within two months Rudy and his .200 batting average were on the bench, Rosen and his broken finger were back at third and Wertz was acquired for first base.

So here was Liddle facing Wertz in a 2-2 tie in the eighth inning. Liddle was ahead in the count, 1-2, when he fired a fastball directly into what they call Wertz's wheelhouse and the result was a blast into the deepest part of center field. Instead of a three-run homer that would have turned Wertz into a hero, the hero's cloak was snatched off Wertz's shoulders and draped around Giants center fielder Willie Mays. With his back to the plate some 440 feet away, Mays caught up with the ball and made an over-the-shoulder catch that stunned 53,000 Manhattanites and 25 guys from Cleveland.

From the dugouts to the press box, it was universally agreed that the ball Wertz hit would have been a home run in every other park, "including Yellowstone," as one New York writer said.

Although Wertz had a terrific World Series, his bad luck continued the next season when he contracted polio. He suffered no paralysis but did miss half of the season.

In the meantime, the inning wasn't over. Pinch hitter Dale Mitchell walked to load the bases and with two outs catcher Jim Hegan launched another blast. This time to left field. Once again, the Indians' dugout came alive, standing, anticipating a grand slam. But the wind blowing in from left field captured the ball in its evil grip and dropped it into the glove of left fielder Monte Irvin, who caught it with his back against the wall.

Lemon was still on the mound as the game continued into the 10th inning, tied. Wertz led off the 10th with a double—his fourth hit of the game—but the Indians stranded two runners and the Giants came to bat in the home half of the 10th.

With two runners on base, Durocher sent his best pinch hitter Dusty Rhodes to the plate against Lemon. A left-handed swinger, Rhodes had batted .341 as a pinch hitter in 1954. Rhodes hacked away at Lemon's first pitch and did not hit it well, barely lifting a lazy fly to right. Cleveland second baseman Avila broke from his position toward the line, thinking he was in the best position to make the catch. But no, the ball hugged the line and it was right fielder Dave Pope's ball. No! It was nobody's ball. The breeze carried it into the first row of seats just inside the foul pole—258 feet from the plate. It was a three-run homer and the Giants won the first game, 5-2.

The next day the game began auspiciously for the Indians. Al Smith led off the game with a home run and the Indians led, 1-0.

But in the fifth Dusty Rhodes pinch hit for Monte Irvin and blooped a single to center that tied the score, 1-1. The Giants scored another run that inning to take a 2-1 lead against Cleveland starting pitcher Early Wynn. Rhodes led off the seventh with another home run, a legitimate one this time, and the

Giants won the second game, 3-1. Wynn and Don Mossi held
the Giants to four hits.

The Indians came home and lost two straight without putting
up much of a fuss. The scores were 6-2 and 7-4 on a Friday and a
Saturday. Eighty thousand Indians fans were left with worthless
tickets for the Sunday game that was never played. At Pat Joyce's
Restaurant on East Ninth Street, the coolers were bulging with
Sunday beer—3.2 percent alcohol in compliance with Ohio's
unique drinking laws of the era. Owner Iggy McIntyre was still
trying to unload it by the next St. Patrick's Day.

Al Rosen, the Indians' great third baseman, said to me once
that the Indians lost the World Series because they lost their
momentum after breaking the Yankees' record for most wins in
a season. They used up their adrenaline going for the record even
after clinching the pennant.

But I'm sticking with my theory. The unique dimensions of
the Polo Grounds cost the Indians the World Series they should
have won.

Tony Horton's Breakdown

TONY HORTON WALKED AWAY from baseball in 1970 and nobody has seen him since.

Tony was a first baseman with power, only 22 years old, when the Indians got him from Boston in a trade for veteran pitcher Gary Bell in 1967. The Red Sox were in a four-way pennant race with Chicago, Detroit and Minnesota and all they needed was another starting pitcher. The deal paid off spectacularly for Boston. Bell's record with Cleveland was 1-5 when he was traded, but with Boston he went 12-8 as the Red Sox won the pennant on the last day. Being traded to a contender was like waking up on Christmas morning in a toy store. The Indians were pathetic at the time. Joe Adcock was listed as the manager but he was more like a zombie.

Bell pops back into Cleveland occasionally, and is a popular fixture at the Indians Fantasy Camp every winter because his outgoing personality lights up a room like a theatre marquee. Former Indians catcher Duke Sims said Bell had other qualities that his teammates admired. "His arm was so sore he couldn't raise it above his shoulder and he never missed a turn," Duke told me.

Tony Horton had tremendous potential. He could have been one of the Indians' all-time best and most popular players. He was tall and Hollywood handsome, a veritable matinee idol, and he did, in fact, come from southern California. By 1969, when he was only 24 years old, Tony led the Indians in homers (27), runs batted in (93) and batting average (.278). The numbers won't dazzle you, but remember this was the famous pitchers' era when offenses went into a deep freeze. Just the names of Sandy Koufax, Bob Gibson and Dennis McLain explain everything.

But Tony had an unhealthy adolescence. As good as he was, he could never satisfy his father. Tony took intensity to a scary level. He gripped the bat as though he were trying to grind it into sawdust. He resurrected memories of Jimmy Piersall, whose career was interrupted by a mental breakdown. Piersall, however, recovered and returned to baseball, playing several years in Cleveland. Tony never recovered.

By 1970 he spent too much time searching for tranquility at the bar of the Blue Grass Motel on Northfield Road, where he lived. He took to the bottle and fell into the welcoming arms of too many femmes fatale. He wasn't getting enough sleep and some of the wires in his brain began to short out.

On June 24, in the first game of a doubleheader in Yankee Stadium, Horton cracked like a maple bat. He looked like a fool when he flailed away at Yankee relief pitcher Steve Hamilton's famous "Folly Floater" and fouled it into the stands behind the plate. The "Folly Floater" was baseball's version of standup comedy. Hamilton lobbed a blooper ball 20 feet high that came down somewhere in the vicinity of home plate. It was the best change-up in baseball. You usually see that pitch on Sunday mornings in a church softball league. When Horton actually swung at it, that was like an engraved invitation to Yankee catcher Thurman Munson. He called for the same pitch and Horton couldn't resist temptation. He swung from his heels again and hit another pop foul behind the plate, which Munson caught for an out.

It was the most humiliating moment of Horton's life. There was no place to hide. He threw his bat away and trudged slowly back to the dugout. He looked around and held out his arms to the crowd of 31,925, whereupon he dropped to his knees and crawled the final step into the dugout. The fans howled, thinking Horton was laughing at himself. Nothing was further from the truth. Inside Horton's soul he was screaming for help.

Barely two months later, Horton's baseball career ended. Some of his teammates sensed that his mental problems were complicated and serious. Others were uncomfortable and avoided him. Even baseball players, with no medical training and certainly no psychiatric knowledge, realized they had a ticking time bomb in their midst.

On Aug. 28 manager Alvin Dark kept Horton out of the lineup. He was in no mental shape to play. That night Tony went back to the Blue Grass and slit his wrists. Motel security discovered him at 5 a.m. sitting in his car bleeding.

Tony was treated in Cleveland for his physical injuries and then he returned to his home near Los Angeles for psychiatric treatment. Cleveland baseball's young star was gone forever.

Over the years many reporters have tried to reach him. Russ Schneider of The Plain Dealer had a brief phone conversation with him in 1973. I tried to reach him in 1979 through his old high school baseball coach in Santa Monica. Tony was working at a bank there. The message came back, "No thank you." New York sportswriter Bill Madden was rebuffed. Tony is now in his 70s and has successfully transformed himself into an urban hermit.

Indians manager Alvin Dark, who died in 2014, blamed himself for ignoring Tony's problems, a subject he approached in a 1980 autobiography called, "When in Doubt Fire the Manager."

Dark was undergoing his own mental problems at the time.

"First, I took Gabe Paul's job away from him," Dark wrote. "Gabe was the general manager and about as good as you'll find in the game, as the Yankees discovered. But in Cleveland I decided I wanted to be manager and general manager. Wear the biggest britches I could. Then having performed this act of lunacy, I systematically alienated just about every member of the press, radio and television in Greater Cleveland."

Dark persuaded Indians owner Vernon Stouffer to give him control over trades, drafting and salary negotiations. It was a disaster. Dark haggled with players over money in the winter and then found it difficult to rally their support when the season started. Dark was a sound manager in 1968, his first year, when the Indians finished third. But he regressed after that. He divorced his first wife and married a second one, whom he took on road trips, which wasn't the way things were done. The fans turned on him.

He became paranoid of a dwarf sportswriter at The Plain Dealer named Dennis Lustig who, Dark alleged, made up critical letters to the editor about him in the weekly "Sound Off" columns. Editing "Sound Off" was a real pain. Addresses and phone numbers were required in order to verify the identities of the writers. Sometimes people were not home and could not be reached. Deadlines, however, were unyielding. Sometimes Dennis just rolled the dice and printed the letters without verification. Many were critical of the Indians manager but respectful and tame, quite unlike the internet posts we read today.

In order to support his allegation, Dark wrote phony letters to "Sound Off" using fictional names which somehow got in the paper. Armed with this proof, he demanded a meeting with sports editor Hal Lebovitz, who then put more pressure on Dennis to verify names and addresses.

As Tony Horton's life was spinning out of control, so was Alvin Dark's. They couldn't get together on Horton's contract and he held out for half of spring training in 1970, which led to his slow start at the beginning of the season. The team was sliding off the rails. "Tony and I never had a harsh word, but I knew he must have taken our salary differences personally," Dark wrote. "I don't necessarily believe it was my fault, but I was the general manager and manager and couldn't give him the objective consideration he deserved. I couldn't help but take it personally."

Dark was fired midway in the 1971 season but went on to have a successful managerial career, including a world championship in Oakland. Dark's second marriage worked out well. They were still together when Alvin died in 2014 at the age of 92. Shortly after leaving Cleveland, Dark wrote apologies for his behavior to Gabe Paul, Hal Lebovitz and other people he harmed. He had a long list.

Game of Threes

(I wrote this piece in April 1981, for The Plain Dealer, which gave me permission to reprint it.)

THEY PLAY THIS GAME all their lives, but they do not know why the distance between the pitcher's rubber and the rear point of home plate is exactly 60 feet, 6 inches, or why the bases are 90 feet apart.

It always has been this way, at least during all of the 20th century, and no one asks: Why?

With few exceptions, baseball is divisible by three. Three strikes. Three outs. Nine innings. Nine men in the traditional lineup. It is called a diamond, but actually it is a square. Each corner is exactly 90 degrees.

The bases are 90 feet apart and are squares, 15 inches on each side and must be at least three inches high.

The ball must be a minimum of nine inches in circumference.

The pitcher's rubber is 24 inches by 6 inches. Bats cannot exceed 42 inches in length and pine tar cannot be applied to a bat beyond 18 inches from the base of the handle.

This is crazy. Every number I have just cited is divisible by three, which you probably already noticed.

Even the players' uniform numbers must be a minimum of 6 inches high. For Major League Baseball, the rules are made by the official playing rules committee. It has nine members.

Home plate is 17 inches wide, but the total of the five sides is 58 inches, which multiplied by three is 174, which was Mark Belanger's batting average in 1967, Dusty Baker's career home runs and Lou Gehrig's runs batted in in 1930. Don't say these are coincidences.

"The reason for this," said Indians infielder Jerry Dybzinski, the Tribe's version of the Shell Answer Man, "is that baseball is a perfectly symmetrical game."

There are nine letters in Dybzinski's name and it is spoken in three syllables. He always pauses three seconds before answering a difficult question.

Why does a curve ball need exactly 60 feet, 6 inches to do its business?

"It is a physical law," speculated Alan Bannister, another Indians infielder. "Notice that when two people start playing catch, even little kids, they keep backing up until there is a comfortable distance between them. Invariably they may be within three inches of being 60 feet, 6 inches from each other. That's when you know you've got it."

Consider the dramatic differences in the game if the pitcher's rubber and the plate were 30 or 40 feet. No hitter would be able to get his bat around on fastballs.

As a result of the ideal 60 feet, 6 inches, the batting average which distinguishes superior batters from the ordinary is .300. The hitter who comes closest to perfection is Eddie Collins, whose lifetime batting average is .333 and who collected 3,313 hits in 24 seasons. He was elected to the Hall of Fame in 1939.

The most perfect pitcher was Warren Spahn with 363 victories.

Babe Ruth wore the number 3 on his uniform and in his best season hit 60 home runs. The year was 1927, naturally. Hall of Famer Stan Musial wore number 6. Ted Williams, who ranks with Ruth as the two greatest left-handed hitters in history, was number 9. Early Wynn, who is in the Hall of Fame with 300 victories, wore 24.

The baseball season once was 154 games, which was not divisible by three. In 1961 the baseball owners smartened up and lengthened it to 162, which is. There are nine letters in the word "expansion."

"If you research Abner Doubleday, who is credited with inventing the game of baseball," said Bannister, "you will find that he shortened his name. Originally, he was Abner Tripleday."

No Good Deed Goes Unpunished

IN THE SPRING OF 1979 a new reporter joined our sports staff at The Plain Dealer. He came from Chicago and he had no car. On the other hand, I had a car I did not need. I was leaving for spring training with the Indians and would be gone for almost two months.

"Take my car until I get home from spring training," I said. "Otherwise, it would just sit in my garage."

I barely knew him, but he was a fellow sportswriter, a teammate and a future drinking buddy.

We opened in Boston that year and when I got home my car wasn't exactly waiting for me in my driveway. I had to track him down to get it back. He had certainly gotten good use of it. It was full of garbage from fast-food joints all over Ohio, much of it from Cincinnati.

"By the way," he said as he handed me my keys. "I got a couple of parking tickets in Euclid. Three or four."

That was all he said about it.

"Fortunately, I don't go to Euclid very often," I said.

I cleaned out my car. The parking tickets weren't there. Time passed. I moved, bought a house and got married. On Saturday of Fourth of July weekend of 1981 our neighbors threw a surprise baby shower for my wife, Maddy. This was our first baby, the first of four. It was likely that later in the evening I would invite everybody back to our house, so I slipped out to buy some provisions.

At that time my sisters and I owned a motor home, a slick, top of the line GMC with an Oldsmobile engine. My sisters had many children and they had many good times in that motor home. I rarely used it, however. It was a monster to navigate around the streets of Lakewood. Because my sisters and their families were out of town on vacation, it was sitting in my driveway. We couldn't leave it unattended anywhere. I hadn't even fired up the engine for over a week so when I went out to get party supplies, I took the motor home just to refresh the battery.

That was the quietest Saturday afternoon of the summer on Detroit Avenue in Lakewood. I carefully parked at a meter and was equally careful later when I pulled away from it. But the rear bumper was bent out at the corner, a souvenir from an earlier mishap, and it caught on the meter's post.

This required some maneuvering to work the bumper free, just enough to catch the attention of a Lakewood cop driving by on routine patrol. What he saw and what I was doing were entirely different. He saw a moving vehicle accident which gave him an excuse to run my name through his computer.

"Euclid has a hold on you. It didn't say why. You'll have to come to the station with me," he said.

The cop permitted me to finish my maneuvering and followed me home, where I parked the motor home in the driveway. I poked my head in the side door and told Maddy I would be back soon after we finished our police business. So, off we went to jail, me in the back seat, like a common criminal.

Lakewood put me in a holding cell where a Lakewood cop told me, "Euclid police are coming to get you. Your bail is $1,000. What'd you do, armed robbery?"

I still didn't know, although those parking tickets came to mind. Soon enough a Euclid squad car arrived to return me to the scene of the crime—in the back seat, naturally. In Euclid they had a cell waiting for me, my own personal cell, and they revealed to me the gravity of my offense. It was those parking tickets, half a dozen of them, all at the same high-rise apartment building on Lake Shore Boulevard, what they called Euclid's Silver Coast. I had never been there but my car had.

Usually, you'll get a notice in the mail about delinquent parking tickets. But not me. Never a word. Maybe because I had moved since the tickets were written two and a half years earlier.

Somewhere along the line I managed to make a couple of phone calls. I don't know how that happened. They hadn't invented cell phones yet. I got word to Maddy that she should go to the shower without me. I'd be along later. Much later. Also, I reached my old sportswriting pal Dick Zunt and asked him to organize a committee to get me out of jail. A few years earlier Dick had managed to get another of our colleagues out of jail in Columbus during the state basketball tournament. He enjoyed practicing law without a license.

My case, however, had a serious complication. It was the $1,000 bail set by Euclid's notorious judge Robert Niccum, whom people called "Stickum Niccum" because of his harsh sentencing. Unless we raised a grand in cash, I'd be sitting in jail until Tuesday. Back in 1981 a thousand dollars was like 10 thousand.

Dick began putting together a network. He involved The Plain Dealer city editor, who tried to put pressure on Euclid politicians to reduce the bail. Only the judge could do that and he was unavailable. Red Pigg, the bartender of the Headliner Saloon, pledged to loan us the receipts of the cash register that night. Most of The Plain Dealer reporters and editors drank there, but a skeleton staff was on duty that night, none of them the reliable heavy drinkers.

In the meantime, Maddy was at the baby shower where everyone asked about me.

"Dan's in jail," she told everyone.

The hostess was our Lakewood City Council president, who called her police chief, the local judge and everyone in Lakewood politics who might help. Nothing was happening. There are certain rules of etiquette, even in politics, which discourage interfering in another town's business.

A Cleveland policeman, who lived down the street, was at the shower. He called a couple of his sergeants, who wisely told him to back off.

Our old friend Bob Daniels, who was sitting in the city editor's chair at The Plain Dealer that night, reached into his reporter's bag of tricks and called someone who knew the judge's bailiff, who found the judge and persuaded him to reduce the bail. In an unexpected display of compassion Judge Niccum slashed it to $300.

That was still a lot of money. There were no ATMs. My relatives were away on vacation. Maddy's family were all at their summer place in Indiana. Nobody I knew even had that kind of dough squirreled away at home, much less in their wallets.

The ball was now in Red Pigg's court, you might say, and it was a slow night at the Headliner. With most of the big drinkers off that night, the dollars trickled in, one at a time. A few printers and circulation truck drivers wandered in, but they didn't linger. The first edition of the big Sunday paper was out and Red still hadn't taken in $300. I was sitting alone in my cell brushing away cobwebs.

Shortly after 10 o'clock a printer threw a dollar on the bar for a shot and a beer and Red reached $300. Dick Zunt grabbed the money and headed for the Euclid jail. The money changed hands, my personal items were returned to me and Dick got me home just before midnight.

"You missed a nice party," my wife said. "How was your night?"

"A quiet evening on the East Side," I said.

To tidy up a few loose ends: We all went to court two weeks later. The fellow who got the tickets wound up paying over a hundred dollars for the tickets and court costs. He should have rented a car.

Stuck in Pittsburgh

I DON'T KNOW WHAT HAL Lebovitz had in mind when he sent me to Pittsburgh to cover a baseball game between the Pirates and the San Francisco Giants in the summer of 1966. It didn't make a lot of sense. It was the third game of a three-game series that was of no interest to our readers in Cleveland. The Giants were in contention for the National League pennant, but the Pirates were going nowhere. Maybe Hal wanted to give me the experience of covering a major-league baseball game out of town on deadline. On the other hand, maybe he wanted to find out if I could read a map.

Hal was our sports editor at The Plain Dealer and I was a young reporter who usually covered things closer to home. However, I did not question the rationale for covering a single game that could have been picked at random. It was time to stretch my wings and this was Forbes Field, a classic ballpark that opened in 1909 and was home to the Pirates for the next 60 years. Babe Ruth hit his last three home runs there in 1935. Several baseball movies were shot there, including one of my all-time black-and-white favorites, the original "Angels in the Out-field," starring Paul Douglas, Janet Leigh and Donna Corcoran as the little girl.

Everything fell into place. I drove to Pittsburgh in the usual way, via the Ohio and Pennsylvania turnpikes. I found Forbes Field, the media gate and the press box and enjoyed the game. I wrote my story and called it in to the paper, dictating it to a rewrite man. Then I attempted to retrace my route and go home. Instead, I discovered Pittsburgh's hidden culture.

This was before every car had a GPS and a compass. I drove tentatively, every other block calling out the window to people on dark street corners, asking them to point me toward the Turnpike. They pointed left, right. Turn here, turn there. Nothing looked familiar. Before long there were no more street lights or traffic lights and the night got darker. It was the darkest night I ever saw.

Suddenly, without warning, I was on a four-lane divided expressway that looked like a turnpike except there were no signs and no toll booths and no other traffic. If this was a turnpike, it could only have been the West Virginia Turnpike because about 20 miles west of Pittsburgh I finally saw a sign that said, to my horror, "Welcome to West Virginia." I got on it and I couldn't get off. This wasn't the West Virginia Turnpike that we know today. That turnpike runs north and south through the mountains and is known as I-77. No, what I stumbled onto was 5 miles of connecting tissue that linked Pennsylvania, West Virginia and Ohio. It traversed over a short stretch of West Virginia real estate that separated Pennsylvania from Ohio. It led me to a bridge that crossed the Ohio River near Steubenville. From the Pittsburgh perspective, that four-lane divided highway across 5 miles of West Virginia landscape easily could have been mistaken for a turnpike.

In hindsight, I'm trying to understand the Pittsburgh mentality. Let's begin with geography. Pittsburgh is a southern city, essentially a suburb of Weirton, West Virginia, which is only 20 miles away. Pittsburgh also falls within the gravitational pull of Wheeling, West Virginia, which is 45 miles away.

That explains why Pittsburgh shares the same language with the entire state of West Virginia. It was natural, then, that when I asked for directions to "the turnpike," their brains went south. The Pennsylvania Turnpike passes Pittsburgh some 20 miles to the north, but that never occurred to the people I ran into that night.

By the way, everybody in Pennsylvania has a quirky way of speaking. In Philadelphia, for example, they have a soft, slurpy speech pattern. John Facenda, the original voice of NFL Films, was from Philadelphia. In the movie, "Silver Linings Playbook," which was set in Philadelphia, none of the actors had the Philadelphia sound. They didn't even try to fake it.

It would be equally difficult to find actors who can speak the Pittsburgh dialect because it cannot be copied. Myron Cope, one of the Steelers radio broadcasters, personified Pittsburgh. He sounded like a guy whose nose had just been smashed in by Jack Lambert. In other words, if you're from Pittsburgh you sound as if you're in constant pain every time you open your mouth. It's as though Mean Joe Greene's size 16 boot is crammed up your anus.

Years ago when they worked together on television at Channel 8, Tim Taylor relentlessly needled Bob Cerminara about his Pittsburgh accent. In the newsroom Taylor called him "Bawb" but never on the air.

No doubt you're wondering, "Where is he going with this?"

That's exactly what I asked back in 1966. I got home at 3:25 a.m., in time for last call at the Lakewood Village Bar. In those days bars didn't close until 3:30 during Daylight Savings Time.

"Why so late? Where'd you go tonight, Cub?" asked bartender Larry Jorgenson, who always called me Cub (for cub reporter).

"Baseball game," I said.

"Same old thing, eh?" said Larry.

Hitchhiking

ON A ZERO-DEGREE DAY in Toledo in 1972, Leon Bibb heard an inner voice that changed his life. A young, poorly paid reporter/photographer at WTOL-TV, Bibb was driving an unmarked station car down West Bancroft Street when he passed a hitchhiker.

"I passed him," said Bibb. "I felt guilty. I knew him from somewhere, I didn't know from where, but he was familiar. An inner voice said, 'Go back and pick him up.' I turned around and went back. He was still there. He got in. He was a college student at the University of Toledo. He noticed the TV camera in the back seat and he recognized me.

"He said, 'My girlfriend's mother asked what happened to you.' Her mother was Ann Walker, the public affairs director of WCMH, the NBC station in Columbus. I called her. She said, 'Funny you should call. We have an opening. Call the news director but wait 30 minutes so I can call him first.'

"The day of my interview it was 10 degrees below zero and I had a dead battery. I called the news director and told him I would be late but I'll be there. I'll take the bus. I did the audition and he said, 'You've got character.' He offered me a job. Three days after I picked up the hitchhiker I was on the air in Columbus, the weekend anchor. I spent six years in Columbus and became the prime time 6 and 11 anchor. I always said the voice I heard was the voice of God."

Over the last 35 years Bibb has become an institution on Cleveland television and an occasional preacher. He preaches a sermon he calls, "The Angel at the Curbside."

My first great hitchhiking adventure began quite differently. It started at McSorley's Ale House, a bar in Lower Manhattan, in October 1957. The voice I heard was a bartender shouting, "Last call."

Let me back up a few hours to the afternoon of Oct. 12 at Municipal Stadium in Philadelphia, where Notre Dame defeated Army, 23-21, on Monte Stickles' field goal in the fourth quarter. The military academies were football powers at the time and Notre Dame's resumption of hostilities with Army after a hiatus of nine years pulsated from coast to coast. Their annual series, which began in 1913, had been suspended for nine years between 1947 and 1957 because its intensity was not in the national interest. Half the country, it seemed, was rooting for Notre Dame and the other half was rooting against Army. If you read that sentence carefully, you will conclude that nobody was on Army's side. And so, on this balmy second Saturday in October, more than 95,000 filled Philadelphia's mammoth stadium to cheer, cheer for old Notre Dame, and I was among them.

Five of us had shoe-horned into a two-door Chevrolet in South Bend, Ind., the day before and driven to Philadelphia, a tedious 670-mile trip. I don't remember who came up with the car, but I do know that my Notre Dame classmate, Ray Mullen, came up with a spare bed in his parents' Philadelphia home for Friday night. Three days and two nights would subsequently pass before I would find solace with a pillow again.

In our Irish-Catholic Notre Dame culture, a dramatic victory such as this required a four-star, eight-column, stop the presses celebration. Steve Barry, a natural leader from Elizabeth, New Jersey, was particularly inspired. "I'll take you to the greatest bar in New York City," he declared.

The five of us squeezed into the Chevy again and headed north. The trip was 100 miles and it took a little over two hours. The car was beginning to smell.

To a freshly turned 19-year-old, New York City on the spur of the moment was more exciting than Vermilion and Geneva-on-the-Lake combined. Everything Barry said was true. McSorley's, located in the West Village of Lower Manhattan, claims to be the oldest continuously operating saloon in New York City, dating to the 1860s, and it is still going strong. Apparently they don't count the Prohibition years. For all I know, McSorley's did not even close during Prohibition. McSorley's seemed to make up its own rules. For example, women were denied entrance until 1970 and I don't know why they put up such a fuss to get in there. The floor was thick with sawdust. It was tidied up every night but it was actually never cleaned. Pictures and placards on the walls dated to the 1800s when Abraham Lincoln drank there. The menu was simple. A six-course meal consisted of six Ritz crackers and bar cheese. The libations were even simpler. McSorley's served only beer and only two kinds of beer, the house lager and the house ale, and you always ordered two at a time. This was not your pedestrian hops and barley joint. You couldn't get a watered down Stroh's or a Carling there. Oh, no. McSorley's industrial-strength beer packed a punch. Over the decades, many people tried to drink McSorley's dry, myself included, but now that we are well into the 21st century no one has come close.

Some time during the evening I became separated from my classmates. When they blinked the lights at closing time I was alone on the sidewalk with a couple of bucks in my pocket, lost in the biggest city in the country.

It was getting cold and luckily I found refuge in a Catholic church. In those days Catholic churches were open all day and night. They were like New Orleans saloons—no locks on the doors. Even petty thieves respected the sanctity of a church. I stretched out in the last pew and caught a few winks, using my rolled-up sports coat for a pillow, until people started arriving for the 6 o'clock Mass. I opened one eye and fulfilled my Sunday obligation. At 7 o'clock I walked out of church and began a 24-hour cross-country odyssey using only my thumb.

At that hour of a Sunday morning there was not much street traffic, but I chatted up the few people who wandered along and got directions to Philadelphia. I planned to retrace my steps. From Philadelphia I would find the Pennsylvania Turnpike and point myself west to Indiana. And that is exactly how it went. It was a beautiful day for traveling, sunny and warm, and I made a spiffy appearance in my button-down shirt, paisley tie and tweedy sport coat. That became my first rule of hitchhiking. Dress up in a tie and sport coat. As for my suitcase and raincoat, they were somewhere on the east coast in the trunk of a two-door Chevy.

After several rides, some short, some shorter, I reached a service plaza on the Pennsylvania Turnpike where a fundamentalist religious family picked me up. I had come across a piece of cardboard that I used for a sign that said simply, "Notre Dame." At service plazas I would hold up my sign and boldly ask strangers for a ride. People were embarrassed to say no. They had good manners in those days. They tended to befriend a clean-cut fellow trying to get back to school. You never read about perverts, muggers and murderers in those days.

My new benevolent family included three generations—two grandparents, two parents and two young children crammed in another two-door Chevy sedan. Everybody in America seemed to drive two-door Chevies. This was an older car, however. It came off the assembly line in the early '50s. They had most of their worldly possessions with them and they had to move boxes around in order to tuck me into a corner of the back seat. According to the new loading plan, I held a box on my lap. We looked like the Joad family in "Grapes of Wrath." Thank God we were not going all the way to California.

I noticed that their car had a radio, and I thought it would be nice if they dialed around and found a pro football game. It was early afternoon and all pro football games started at 2 o'clock. I figured that we were within range of the Philadelphia Eagles, Washington Redskins or Pittsburgh Steelers radio networks. The Eagles, as a matter of fact, were in Cleveland playing the Browns. But, no, they found a radio preacher somewhere on the AM dial. Two o'clock rolled around and the preacher kept preaching.

Not long afterward the father turned off the radio and my

mind raced. I wanted to ask if we could listen to a pro football game, but there were etiquette issues. I had been politely silent up to that point. I stayed out of their family business. In fact, everybody had been quiet. They seemed to take the Sabbath very seriously, more seriously than Irish Catholics. Maybe they considered pro football on Sunday a mortal sin. I had read about people like that. Normal Protestants enjoy pro football as much as anybody, including Catholics, but I knew nothing about religious fundamentalists.

While I was internalizing this, the subject became moot. The grandmother came up with a Bible. She plunged right into the Old Testament and began reading aloud. I had already been to the 6 o'clock Mass after a night of drinking and I was tired. I fell asleep somewhere between the major prophets Ezekiel and Daniel.

The radio issue aside, these were truly kind people. They woke me up and dropped me off at the last service plaza before they exited the turnpike. There should be a special place in heaven for folks like this. For others, I give you the Muny Parking Lot.

My next ride came from a long-distance trucker in a rig with about 20 forward gears, and he used most of them in the mountainous region of Pennsylvania. He was a young guy, probably in his 30s, and apparently he wanted company because he kept up a steady stream of chatter as he slammed the transmission in and out of gear like a kid driving a hot rod. I stayed awake and listened in case he dropped his transmission and we plummeted out of control down the side of a mountain.

Along the way he came up on another trucker whom he seemed to recognize. He said hello by ramming him from behind. It was dark now and the poor devil in front of us must have thought the guy playing bumper cars with him was a total lunatic. My guy must have had a lighter load or a stronger engine because the guy in front was unable to pull away. The ramming went on for quite a while until the guy in front got off the turnpike and my guy pulled into a service plaza for a nap. That was fine with me.

It was getting late and it was getting cold and there were fewer cars on the turnpike, but it was a good trip as long as my sign and I worked our way from one service plaza to the next. Unfortunately, about 4 o'clock in the morning my driver forgot the rules. I had fallen asleep and was awakened by a guy saying, "This is as far as I'm going. You can get out here."

He was off the turnpike and I found myself at a desolate toll booth about 60 miles from South Bend. Toll booth clerks were not sympathetic to hitchhikers, so I walked down to the end of the entrance ramp in total darkness hoping to catch the attention of a car just entering the turnpike before it got up to turnpike speed. The Indiana Toll Road had been open barely more than a year, and lighting the entrance and exit ramps had not occurred to them yet. After two hours of shivering in 40-degree temperature, one compassionate soul stopped and delivered me the final 60 miles. However, he was going to Chicago so he dropped me off on the berm of the main toll road and I walked the final 2 miles to Stanford Hall.

Allowing for some minor inconveniences, such as hunger, thirst, cold, sleep deprivation, lack of comfort, uncertainty and humiliation—like riding the New York Central in those days—I felt triumphant. I had just traveled from Lower Manhattan to South Bend, Ind., on $2. My thumb was exhausted.

Thereafter I rode my thumb back and forth to college several times, even though I could take the New York Central between Cleveland and South Bend for only $10 each way because my father worked on the railroad. But my thumb was more reliable. The New York Central sometimes ran hours behind schedule and the cars were dirty and cold.

Later I hitchhiked in a blizzard from Cleveland to Fort Hood, Texas. I hopped military flights from Air Force bases in Texas to various parts of the country—not necessarily where I wanted to go. One Christmas I rode an Army helicopter from Texas to eastern Pennsylvania—not my preferred destination. I attempted to mooch rides on military planes to an old pal's wedding in Lexington, Kentucky, but got no farther than Nashville because all the military planes were going the other way, supporting James Meredith's enrollment at the University of Mississippi.

Now, of course, I take commercial flights—and there's a good chance I'll be deposited where I do not want to go.

Miami's Greatest Team

I TOOK THE DWARF WITH me to Orlando, Florida, to cover the 1974 Tangerine Bowl—Miami of Ohio versus Georgia. It was a big mistake. Bringing the dwarf, I mean.

Dennis Lustig was short. One night between editions we stretched him out on the sports copy desk at The Plain Dealer and measured him with a printer's ruler. He turned out to be 44 inches long, barely more than three and a half feet, which was short even for a dwarf. He was hired to answer the phones in the sports department, but his arms were too short to reach the old-fashioned phone boxes on each desk, so that wouldn't work. His legs were too short to run for coffee, so that wouldn't work, either. When they were out of options they made a reporter out of him. It was debated whether that worked.

Over time he became my buddy, my drinking buddy. He was everybody's drinking buddy. Back in 1967 I took him with me to Dallas to cover a Browns-Cowboys playoff game. The details of that trip are in my first book, "Crazy, with the Papers to Prove It." I must have been out of my mind to invite him to join me in Florida seven years later for the big college bowl game because it certainly diverted me from the purpose of my trip.

That was the heyday of Miami football. In fact, it might have been the high point of Mid-American Conference football. During the eight-year contract with the Tangerine Bowl, MAC schools won six of them. Toledo, with Chuck Ealey at quarterback, won three straight from 1969 to '71, crushing the Southern Conference champion each year. Ealey led Toledo to 35 straight victories and later starred in the Canadian Football League, where he was named the most valuable player in the Grey Cup game.

Miami won three straight from 1973 to '75 against slightly tougher competition. In 1973, with Bill Mallory coaching, Miami beat Florida, 16-7, a victory that propelled Mallory to the head coaching job at Colorado.

Dick Crum succeeded Mallory and the Redskins got even better. (Miami was called the Redskins in those days.) In its next two Tangerine Bowl appearances, Miami manhandled Georgia, 21-10, and dominated South Carolina, 20-7.

In those days Miami avoided nobody. The Redskins would play anybody any place, usually on the road. Early in the 1974 season Miami went down to Lexington and beat Kentucky in their brand new stadium. Later Miami travelled to West Lafayette, Indiana, where Purdue escaped with a tie when Miami's winning touchdown pass was nullified by a penalty. It was the only blemish on its record.

"It was an offensive holding call on the other side of the field, nowhere near the ball. That penalty wouldn't even be called today," Crum said not long ago.

The Tangerine Bowl should not be confused with the Orange Bowl. No, the Tangerine Bowl Stadium in Orlando held only 18,000 people. The game wasn't even on conventional network television. It was on a southern regional independent network.

I had covered some monster bowl games by then, such as the 1969 Cotton Bowl when Texas beat Notre Dame for the national championship and the 1973 Sugar Bowl when Notre Dame beat Alabama for the national championship. The guy sitting next to me in East Lansing for the 10-10 tie between Notre Dame and Michigan State in 1966 was New York sportswriter Jimmy Breslin, a giant of journalism at the time.

But this one was special to me because I had known Dick Crum since his first head coaching job at Mentor High School. He was a studious, classy guy a couple of years older than me. He always wore tweedy, wool sport coats and Ivy League ties. He looked like a literature professor at Dartmouth. He always returned my phone calls.

The guy sitting next to me in the press box in Orlando that

night was not a giant of journalism or a giant of anything. He was Dennis Lustig, nursing a severe hangover.

It was an eventful week up to that point. Two days before the game the independent television network pre-produced the introduction of the starting lineups, which meant that Crum had to name his starting quarterback, something he preferred not to do. Miami had alternated two distinctly different quarterbacks— Steve Sanna, a passing quarterback from Shaker Heights, and Sherman Smith, a powerful runner from Youngstown.

"Sherman Smith had been our starter for the last four or five games," Crum recalled. "With Sherman Smith and our running backs Randy Walker and Rob Carpenter, we had a pretty good load right there."

Smith became a running back in the NFL for eight years. Carpenter carried the ball for 10 years in the NFL. Walker turned immediately to coaching and eventually was the head coach at Northwestern until he died of a heart attack at age 52.

It was clear to many people that Sherman Smith was the starter, but Georgia coach Vince Dooley wasn't certain and Crum wasn't going to tell him.

"Five minutes after we record our starting lineups, Dooley is going to know," said Crum.

So he introduced Steve Sanna as his starter.

My dear friend Dick Zunt was also there covering the game for The Plain Dealer, something he did for years. Dick always turned it into a Christmas vacation for his wife, Mary, and their four young children. Dick's idea of family vacations usually included football, basketball or baseball games or track meets. For many years Mary went along with it.

The day before the game Dennis and I joined the Zunt family for an outing at Disney World. Our game credentials included free passes. I've had better ideas.

Dennis abhorred little children because in their innocence they often walked up directly to him and asked, "Do you want to play?" Sometimes they only circled him and stared.

He would snarl, growl and go berserk, frightening the children by the dozens. Where will you find more children than Disney World? No place, especially five days before Christmas. Chaos was our constant companion. Dennis rented a stroller for himself and climbed in. I pushed him around the park like a rickshaw driver with a very unhappy customer.

When we got back to the hotel, Dennis was angry and thirsty. He found refuge in the bar, where there were no children. Sufficiently insulated, Dennis began pounding them down. By the end of the night Dennis was seen hurling his Gideon bible off his second floor balcony and into the swimming pool. I can understand his contempt for the New Testament but I couldn't reconcile his attitude toward the Old Testament, his being Jewish and all.

Anyway, Miami totally dominated Georgia, 21-10. Miami's team came almost exclusively from Ohio—players who were overlooked by Ohio State and other Big Ten schools. Ohio high schools, it should be noted, were bursting at the seams and producing an abundance of football players. Even here at home, people did not comprehend the quality of play in the Mid-American Conference.

When the final Associated Press college rankings came out a few days later, there was Miami (Ohio) ranked 10th in the nation, the highest ranking ever for a Mid-American Conference school.

That's how it always appeared in the Sunday paper in agate type—Miami (Ohio)—to differentiate it from Miami of Florida. Our Miami, the one in Oxford, Ohio, a public college in a football conference with other public colleges, always was comfortable in its own skin. Miami of Florida, a private school in Coral Gables, has its own story for another day.

Bob Gain Took a Bullet

BOB GAIN DID MANY brave things in his life. He led a rebellion against his tyrannical college coach Paul "Bear" Bryant. He defied an Air Force colonel. Just for the hell of it, he flew on a bombing mission over North Korea. In 13 professional football seasons he backed down against nobody. But when he challenged his wife, he almost died. That's when he should have shut up and backed down. That, however, is not in his DNA. He's well into his 80s and he hasn't mastered the art of shutting up.

Let's begin the Bob Gain story on Christmas Eve of 1995 when the Browns' old defensive tackle stepped out to run some errands.

"I stopped in a couple of bars on the way home," he admits.

It was well into the evening and Bob was half-loaded when he arrived home to his wife, Kitty, who was growing angry and impatient. While Bob was in the bars, she, too, was sampling the healing waters at home. They were both overly involved in the Christmas spirits.

"I'd like to shoot you," an irate Kitty said to him.

"Well then, why don't you?" said Bob.

She couldn't think of a reason why not, so she went into the bedroom of their Timberlake home and got Bob's .45 out of the nightstand drawer and returned to the family room. At 6 feet, 3 inches and 250 pounds Bob presented a target that was difficult to miss, and she didn't. She put a bullet into his chest near his heart. Why a man of that size needed a gun next to his bed is a question with no logical answer.

Bob slumped into a chair and said, "Call 911."

"She went into the kitchen and I didn't hear anything. I didn't know if she was calling 911 or reloading so I went in there. She was actually calling 911. I sat down in a kitchen chair and they came and got me in an ambulance," Bob recalled.

He spent the next three months on the critical list at Metro General Hospital, where they cut him open and discovered his insides were scrambled. The repair job was massive. It was like putting in a new kitchen. Lowe's would have charged 20 grand and would have done it in half the time. Kitty, meanwhile, was facing a prison term. At one point the Lake County judge wanted to put her away for five years.

"They can't do that," said Bob. "Who's gonna take care of me? I've been shot, you know."

Bob called on his friends to write letters to the judge, pleading for compassion and leniency. The outpouring of support softened the judge's heart. He took into account that they were both 65 years old and they needed each other, improbable as it may have seemed.

It was a wise decision. Kitty spent six months at a halfway house called Women's Freedom House in the old convent at St. Clement Catholic Church in Lakewood, which Bob enthusiastically supported. As he regained his strength he raised $100,000 for amenities and necessities there. Needless to say, the nuns were gone. At one time the convent was bursting at the seams with nuns, my nuns, the ones I had in grade school at St. Clement. For the most part they were sweet and comforting. Only one could have been charged with assault and I told you about her in the forward of this book. When the last nuns moved out, I'm guessing they left behind their good karma, which must have rubbed off on Kitty.

As I write this, neither Bob nor Kitty has had a drink since that fateful Christmas so many years ago. In fact, they have been like lovebirds on an endless second honeymoon.

"We don't talk about the past. That's water over the dam," Bob says. "I love her more than ever. I'll always love her until the day I die. I'm already living on borrowed time."

As a constant reminder of his love, Bob carries the .45 caliber slug on his key chain. It tells him to come straight home.

Bob was born in Akron on June 21, 1929. When he was in the sixth grade his father died and his mother moved them to Weirton, West Virginia, where Bob became a high school football star. He was recruited by every college football power east of the Mississippi River and it came down to Notre Dame and the University of Kentucky.

"Moose Krause recruited me for Notre Dame. He said I could probably play by my junior year and I'd probably start in my senior year," Bob recalled.

He didn't like the time frame. "What would I do my first two years, pray?" he wondered.

The Kentucky coach was Paul "Bear" Bryant, who was just starting his college career and was building the Kentucky program from the ground up. Texas A&M and Alabama were in his distant future. He promised Bob that he would start for four years at Kentucky and that's exactly what happened. Bob became a two-time All-American. As a senior he won the Outland Trophy which went to the outstanding interior lineman in the country and he was the first-round draft choice of the Green Bay Packers.

In Bob's junior year, which was the 1949 season, Kentucky was invited to the Orange Bowl, where they played Santa Clara and where Bear Bryant established his reputation as a madman. Preparation for the Orange Bowl was like boot camp.

"He worked us to death. We'd get up at 6 or 6:30 every morning. We'd scrimmage twice a day," Bob said. "When we went to Miami, he told us, the 'hard work' is over. He ran us just as hard in Miami. He thought we ate like pigs for Christmas dinner, so we ran 12, 15, 20 wind sprints after practice. We had brand new wool uniforms. In the heat of Miami we ran out of gas in the second half and we got beat, 21-13. We should have won easily. I weighed myself after the game. I lost 22 pounds in a week."

The following year Kentucky took a 10-0 record into its final game, which was at Tennessee on Saturday of Thanksgiving weekend, the day of the famous 1950 blizzard. In Cleveland we awakened to two feet of snow. It was just as bad in Columbus, where Ohio State and Michigan combined for 45 punts in a game they called the Snow Bowl. Michigan won, 9-3, with no first downs, scoring a touchdown and a safety on two blocked punts.

In Knoxville, Tennessee, the temperature plummeted to 8 degrees, catching Kentucky in summer shortsleeved uniforms.

"I was never that cold ever again, not even on the coldest winter days in Cleveland," Bob recalled.

"We lost, 7-0, and after the game Bear came in the locker room and said, 'We can go back to the Orange Bowl.' I was the co-captain and the spokesman and I told Bear to leave the locker room and we would take a vote.

"When we called him back in, I said we would play one team, Oklahoma. 'What if we can't get Oklahoma?' he said. 'Then the season's over,' I said. He left and came back in a little while. 'You've got Oklahoma in the Sugar Bowl,' he said."

Oklahoma had just been declared national champion because in those days the national championship was determined after the regular season. Bowl games were not considered.

"So we would play Oklahoma, but there were other things on our minds. We said there would be new ground rules," Bob continued. "There would be no scrimmaging and no three-on-one blocking the final week. Furthermore, we would follow the printed practice schedule. And one other thing, everybody goes home for three days at Christmas."

The great Bear Bryant agreed to all the terms, even though his entire system—body, mind and soul—probably was rebelling. He understood that his players were serious. At least, his best player was. Kentucky, which was a 13-point underdog, went on to beat the national champion Oklahoma Sooners, 13-7, and end Oklahoma's 31-game winning streak. The Kentucky players took one more vote. They gave Bear Bryant the game ball.

The NFL draft was held three weeks later and Bob was the fourth player selected, chosen by Green Bay.

"What will it take to make you happy?" the Green Bay general manager asked Bob.

"Eight thousand dollars," said Bob.

"We'll give you seven thousand," said the man from Green Bay.

"Why did you ask me what would make me happy?" Bob said. "That doesn't make me happy."

He signed with Ottawa of the Canadian Football League for $9,100 and helped the Rough Riders win the 1951 Grey Cup, the CFL championship trophy. They loved Bob in Canada and Bob liked Canada. They made good beer. After one year in Canada, however, Bob came back to the States and signed with the Browns, who had traded with Green Bay for his rights.

Bob and Kitty got married in 1952 before his first season with the Browns. Bob played well and the Browns won their conference but lost the NFL championship game to Detroit. Bob's major concern, however, was the Korean War. He had taken Air Force ROTC at Kentucky and was a lieutenant just waiting to be called up. He went on active duty in January 1953. In those days every normal male with a heartbeat was subject to military service.

There were several deals proposed to make Bob available to play football for the Browns on weekends while he was on Air Force duty, and Bob didn't like any of them. Browns coach Paul Brown had friends in high places who could arrange to fly Bob to Browns games every Sunday.

"Absolutely not," said Bob. "All those writers in New York and Philadelphia would raise hell if they found the government was flying me around to play football."

Bob was assigned to Sewart Air Force Base in Smyrna, Tennessee, where the commanding officer desired his services on the base football team. In that era most military installations, home and overseas, fielded football teams. Some base commanders actually took those games seriously. The football scene in the movie "M*A*S*H" was not far off the truth. Once again, Bob refused, and the colonel didn't like being rejected.

"The next day I got orders to Korea," he said. "If anybody said I got preferential treatment, I'll kick their ass. I'll serve my country."

Bob landed at a bomber base. He wasn't a pilot. He was on ground duty. Air Force cockpits weren't big enough to accommodate people of Bob's size. But he had a yen for the wild blue yonder. Bob buddied up with a B-26 bomber pilot who invited him along for a ride, if that's what you want to call a bombing run.

"I sat in the co-pilot's chair and my head was up against the roof of the plane. When we got back I had a stiff neck," Bob said.

He was lucky he wasn't shot down. Everybody involved was also lucky to avoid discipline, especially since the colonel learned of the ride-along, which was against regulations.

Bob missed the Browns' entire 1953 season and he also would have missed the entire 1954 campaign. His discharge date was January 4, 1955. Furthermore, Bob was not certain he would ever return to the Browns. The NFL and Canadian Football League were still waging war over players and it was driving up salaries, more so in Canada than in the States. In letters and phone calls to Kitty he addressed his interest in returning to the Ottawa Rough Riders.

All that Canada talk made Kitty uncomfortable. She finally revealed to Bob that every week while he was overseas, Paul Brown and his wife, Katie, called her to check on her. Paul even sent her money. That information changed everything. "I can't go to Canada now," Bob said. He was coming home to Cleveland.

He counted down the days leading up to his discharge in January 1955. The Air Force allocated the final 30 days for processing out, which actually took only a couple of days. Bob also had accumulated 37 furlough days. He reckoned that he would be available to play the final two games of the 1954 season plus the championship game.

"I had to start getting in shape," Bob recalled. "I was smoking a pack a day and drinking every night. So I played on the base team in Japan. It got me in shape."

The colonel finally got his man.

Bob played in the final two games of the 1954 season plus the championship game. The Browns crushed the Detroit Lions, 56-10, and the team included him in their share of the playoff money. "They voted me half a share," he said.

Over the next 10 years Gain was one of the greatest Browns of all time, a list that includes some of the most glorious names in the game's history. He was selected for five Pro Bowls. In 1957 he was named the NFL's outstanding defensive player and was honored at a banquet in Los Angeles attended by 1,000 people. The MC was Bob Hope.

"They had me sitting on the dais next to some big government guy from Washington, D.C.," said Bob.

Bob has a super-sized picture of the crowded ballroom which shows him sitting next to Earl Warren, chief justice of the United States Supreme Court. I'm sure their conversation was scintillating. It makes me think of a line Bob tossed at Paul Brown.

"Hey, Paul. Do you know how to spell 'boss' backward?" Without waiting for an answer, Bob said, "Double s-o-b." Then he walked away.

Bob Gain's pro football career ended in the fourth game of the 1964 season when he broke his leg against the Dallas Cowboys. His leg was still in a cast late in the season when he was asked to speak at a Touchdown Club luncheon.

"You're really scraping the bottom of the barrel, getting a one-legged speaker," Bob began.

Later he served two separate terms as president of the Cleveland Touchdown Club, in an era when it was one of the most prestigious organizations in the country.

In 1980 he was inducted into the College Football Hall of Fame, which leads me to the nagging question: Why isn't he in the Pro Football Hall of Fame in Canton? Several years ago I complained about this to the president of the Hall of Fame.

"He falls into the category of the very good," was the reply.

I thought that was merely an expression. Later I learned that there actually is a category called the Hall of Very Good. The Professional Football Researchers Association has compiled such a list and Bob is on it. He was "enshrined" in 2010. That's not good enough. Bob Gain was more than that.

I have my personal list of former Browns whom I consider Hall of Famers in waiting. Besides Bob Gain it includes wide receiver Gary Collins and defensive tackle Jerry Sherk, neither of whom is even in the Hall of Very Good. They're at least Very Good. Collins, who caught 70 touchdown passes in a 10-year career, also was the Browns' punter for six of those years and he once led the league in punting. He did two jobs and got paid for one.

Other former Browns who are listed in the Hall of Very Good include coach Blanton Collier, offensive tackle Lou Rymkus, linebacker Lou Saban, guard Jim Ray Smith, offensive tackle Dick Schafrath, wide receiver Mac Speedie, defensive back Erich Barnes and guard Gene Hickerson, who later was voted into the big one, the Hall of Fame.

So where are Greg Pruitt, John Wooten, Michael Dean Perry and Clay Matthews? We're playing a dangerous game here. You might say, "Where are Thom Darden, Doug Dieken, Clarence Scott and Frank Minnifield?"

And your father might say, "Where are Dub Jones, Ray Renfro, Walt Michaels and Tony Adamle?"

Draft Choices

WORLD WAR II WAS catastrophic for most people, but not for Paul Brown. He did not permit the trivialities of war to distract him from his primary mission. No, he used the war to build a pro football dynasty in Cleveland.

Brown, who had been head football coach at Ohio State from 1941-43, was commissioned a lieutenant in the U. S. Navy in 1944 and assigned to coach football at Great Lakes Naval Training Station 30 miles north of downtown Chicago on Lake Michigan. That was good duty. Many college coaches found themselves on the high seas or in ground battles when they served their country. Woody Hayes, for example, served for five solid years on warships in the Pacific and came out of the navy as a lieutenant commander. Frank Leahy of Notre Dame was a recreation director for submariners on the islands of Tarawa, Guam, Midway and Saipan in the Pacific.

Paul "Bear" Bryant was a 28-year-old vagabond assistant college football coach with a wife and a 5- year-old child when Pearl Harbor was attacked. The next day he enlisted in the Navy. His first overseas assignment as a naval officer was on the troop ship USS Uruguay in the Mediterranean off North Africa. Two hundred soldiers and sailors were lost when the Uruguay was rammed by another vessel. Near the end of the war Bryant was assigned to the Pre-Flight training center at the University of North Carolina where he started a football team in 1944. The next year Bryant was out of the Navy and was handed his first college head coaching job at the University of Maryland. The nucleus of that Maryland team was made up of players he coached at North Carolina Pre-Flight. To refresh your memory, this is the same Bear Bryant who later coached at Kentucky, Texas A&M and Alabama.

As for Paul Brown, they gave him a train ticket to Chicago. Great Lakes Naval Training Station provided him a marvelous vantage point to scout talent that would later play for the Browns. Brown built his team through the draft, but not the football draft. He built it through the military draft.

Here's how World War II affected sports in America. Virtually every physically able male human being between ages 20 and 30 was in the military, except for those already working in critical industries, such as airplane factories and tank plants. Even the nation's most famous athletes were called. Ted Williams was flying Corsairs off aircraft carriers in the Pacific. Not far away on the battleship USS Alabama was Bob Feller, shooting down enemy planes. Warren Spahn was in the infantry in Europe. Here at home there was such a paucity of baseball talent that in 1945 the St. Louis Browns even employed a one-armed outfielder named Pete Gray, who hit an unremarkable .218 in 77 games but collected five hits in a doubleheader in Yankee Stadium.

Football was similarly affected. The National Football League barely stayed in business. Teams didn't have enough players to fill out their rosters. The Pittsburgh Steelers and Philadelphia Eagles actually merged for one season as the "Steagles," playing two games in Pittsburgh and four in Philadelphia. The Cleveland Rams did not even field a team in 1943 when Rams owner Dan Reeves was in the Army. The Rams lost money every year and had moved during the war from 80,000-seat Cleveland Stadium to comparatively tiny League Park.

For the Rams, matters turned from bad to worse. With the 11th pick in the first round of the 1944 college draft, the Rams chose running back Anthony Butkovich, who was a star at two colleges—first at Illinois and then at Purdue, where he set the Big Ten scoring record with 78 points in seven games. Butkovich was a corporal in the Marines and was shot and killed at Okinawa on April 18, 1945. It was speculated that Butkovich was the victim of friendly fire, shot accidentally by another member of his platoon when he forgot the password. No one knows for sure.

Two years earlier the 1939 Heisman Trophy winner Nile Kinnick, from Iowa, lost his life when his plane went down during a training mission in the Gulf of Paria off the coast of Venezuela. Because the oil pump broke, the engine on his F4F trainer froze 4 miles shy of reaching the flight deck of the aircraft carrier Lexington. Neither Kinnick nor his plane was ever recovered.

College football also was devastated. Players were yanked out of college and, before going overseas, were assigned to training bases in this country. Believing that it was good for troop morale, the military bases fielded football teams. With most of the college and NFL players in the service, the military teams were integrated into the college schedules. Not only did the military teams play the colleges, they beat them. The Army, Navy and Marine bases were bundled with the colleges in the wire service polls and in 1943 Notre Dame's 14-13 victory at home over Iowa Pre-Flight determined the national championship. The Fighting Irish finished first and Iowa Pre-Flight was second. Curiously, the following week Great Lakes handed the Irish their only loss, 19-14, scoring on a desperation pass with 33 seconds left. It did not affect Notre Dame's hold on first place but it propelled Great Lakes up to sixth in the final rankings.

The following year military teams comprised more than half of the Associated Press top 20. Here are the final rankings for the 1944 season:

1. U. S. Military Academy (West Point)
2. Ohio State
3. Randolph Field
4. U. S. Naval Academy (Annapolis)
5. Bainbridge Military Base
6. Iowa Pre-Flight
7. Southern Cal
8. Michigan

9. Notre Dame
10. Fourth Air Force
11. Duke
12. Tennessee
13. (tie) Georgia Tech
13. Norman Pre-Flight
15. Illinois
16. El Toro Marines
17. Great Lakes Naval Training
18. Fort Pierce
19. St. Mary's Pre-Flight
20. Second Air Force

Here's what the colleges were dealing with. Purdue's 1943 roster was typical—26 Marines, 9 Navy and 9 civilians. Purdue went undefeated and won the Big Ten. By the end of the war colleges offered only 18 football scholarships a year because many of their players already were on scholarship—military scholarships.

In September 1944, the Chicago Tribune's influential sports editor Arch Ward put together the All-America Football Conference to rival the crippled National Football League. His plan was to go active as soon as the war ended. Maybe Ward was a visionary, but more likely he was an opportunist.

Ward set out to sell franchises in his new league and he found buyers. The Cleveland franchise went to Arthur B. "Mickey" McBride, who grew up in Chicago but moved to Cleveland where he made his fortune with horse racing wires, real estate and taxi cabs. Next, McBride needed a coach. Frank Leahy of Notre Dame, who was still leading jumping jacks on Guam, was considered. McBride was a fervent fan of the Fighting Irish. His son, Artie, was enrolled at Notre Dame at the time. But none other than Notre Dame All-American Creighton Miller advised McBride that Leahy was a bad fit for war-hardened adults returning from the service.

"I know. I played for him," said Miller.

So McBride settled on Brown, who won the national championship in 1942 at Ohio State, and was expected to return to Columbus as soon as the war was over.

On Feb. 8, 1945, however, Brown accepted McBride's offer to coach the Cleveland team, which did not yet have a name. Brown's salary was $17,500, double what he had been making at Ohio State, and he was made a minor owner. He went on the payroll immediately, even though he was still a full-time naval officer and actively engaged in coaching the Great Lakes team. The war was winding down in Europe but it was still raging in the Pacific.

Brown then began one of the most famous construction jobs in football history. He built himself a team. Let it be known that the Browns did not come into this world in the usual way, to borrow a line from Harry Chapin.

Brown knew quarterback Otto Graham well—too well. In 1941, Otto's sophomore year at Northwestern, he passed for two touchdowns as Northwestern handed Paul Brown's Ohio State team its only loss of the season. In his senior year when he led Northwestern to victory over both Ohio State and Great Lakes Naval Training Station, Graham was the Big Ten MVP and finished third in the Heisman Trophy voting. Graham was a stranger to nobody. In fact, he had been drafted by the Detroit Lions in 1944. The NFL draft meant nothing to Paul Brown and the rest of the fledgling All-America Football Conference, however. The AAFC did not recognize the NFL draft. In fact, they did not recognize the NFL at all. The newly formed AAFC had no rules to follow. In the vernacular at the time, the AAFC was an outlaw league and the Browns were an outlaw team.

Paul Brown located Graham in North Carolina where he was in pilot training and still playing football for the base team coached by Bear Bryant. It was at North Carolina that Graham had his first experience with the T formation. Most colleges were still playing the single wing. For Graham, this was like football graduate school.

With Brown still tethered to his naval base, he sent assistant coach Johnny Brickels on the road to sign players. Brickels, a civilian operating out of offices in the Leader Building in Cleveland, was the first assistant coach Brown hired and his first recruiting visit was to Graham at Chapel Hill, North Carolina.

"We are offering you $7,500 per year to play football," said Brickels. Then he spelled out the details. The war was almost over in Europe. Germany was collapsing. But it was still raging in the Pacific. No one knew how long the Japanese would hold out. "You will receive a monthly stipend of $250 a month until the war is over. Is this acceptable?" said Brickels as he handed Graham a contract.

Graham was jubilant. He was the highest-paid ensign in the navy.

Brown had a list of players he coached at Massillon High School, Ohio State and Great Lakes. His list also included those he coached against. He mailed contracts to Lou Groza and Dante Lavelli, two players whom Brown had recruited to Ohio State. Lavelli played on Brown's 1942 national championship team and then went into the service. Groza played on the freshman team and then joined the army. Brown put them on the payroll while they were overseas.

People at Ohio State were infuriated. Groza had three years of eligibility remaining. Lavelli had two years. The relationship between Brown and Ohio State athletic director Lynn St. John was irreparably destroyed. Brown was considered greedy and disloyal.

"Their classes have already graduated," Brown rationalized. "It's time for them to go to work."

Brickels packed his big suitcase and went on the road. Brown had a roster assembled before the other teams in the All-America Conference had coaches, before some even had names.

In 1946 Brown signed tackle Jim Daniell, who had been all-pro the previous year with the Chicago Bears. Daniell had played on Brown's 1941 team at Ohio State.

"He gave me $9,000 plus another thousand to be his first

captain," Daniell told me years later. "I was making three thousand a year with the Bears."

Halfback Edgar "Special Delivery" Jones also defected from the Chicago Bears.

Brown virtually eviscerated the Cleveland Rams, who had won the NFL championship in December 1945, and three months later moved to Los Angeles. Brown stole halfbacks Don Greenwood and Tom Colella and center Mike "Mo" Scarry from the Rams.

Brown also pried loose powerful tackle Chet Adams from the Rams with an assist from federal judge Emerich B. Freed. Rams owner Dan Reeves claimed Adams was irreplaceable and filed a lawsuit to keep him, pointing out that Adams had actually signed a contract to play with the Rams in the 1946 season. Adams, who grew up in Cleveland's Slavic Village and played at South High, had no intention of going to Los Angeles. "I signed with the Cleveland Rams, not the Los Angeles Rams," he said.

"You're right," said Judge Freed. "You are free to stay."

The Browns were among the first pro sports teams to hire black players, a full year before Jackie Robinson and Larry Doby broke baseball's color barrier. Brown signed fullback Marion Motley and defensive lineman Bill Willis, black players whom the coach ran across earlier in his coaching career. Willis played for Brown at Ohio State. The paths of Brown and Motley had intersected twice already. Brown coached against Motley in high school when he played at Massillon's arch-rival Canton McKinley and then Motley played for Brown at Great Lakes.

Paul Brown was supposed to be the smartest man in football in the 1940s and '50s when his Cleveland Browns played in 10 straight league championship games, winning seven of them, and the college draft had almost nothing to do with it. Brown didn't build his dynasty through the draft, the way it's supposed to be done now. No, he built the original 1946 Browns by stealing and cajoling players away from everybody else. Paul Brown was pro football's safecracker. Brown gave signing bonuses to players who were still in military uniforms actively involved in World War II. And he signed black players at a time when all pro sports in America were virtually lily-white. Hardly any of them were strangers. Seven of the original 33 played for him at Ohio State. He coached against others. Lin Houston played for Brown at both Massillon and Ohio State. Two years later another of Brown's former Massillon players, Horace Gillom, made the team. Six of the 33 eventually were inducted into the Pro Football Hall of Fame.

Assistant coaches were hired in a similar fashion. Fritz Heisler, who became the Browns line coach, played for Paul at Massillon.

The connection between Brown and Blanton Collier began at Great Lakes. After the war Brown brought Collier to Cleveland as his number one assistant coach. Sadly, their friendship ended in 1963 when Brown was fired and Collier succeeded him as head coach of the Browns.

The All-America Football Conference lasted only four years, and the Browns won all four championships with a cumulative record of 52-4-3. When the league collapsed, three of the AAFC's seven teams were merged into the National Football League. They were the Browns, San Francisco 49ers and Baltimore Colts.

Otto Graham:
A Kinder Era

IF ANYBODY EVER HAD the credentials to play the big man on campus, it was Otto Graham, who set the gold standard for quarterbacks.

He was born for it. Literally. On the day he was born in 1921 Graham weighed 14 pounds, 12 ounces. His mother must have gasped when she finally caught her breath. A notation on a picture in his baby book says that at six weeks old he weighed 20 pounds, whereupon I imagine both parents gasped.

Everything about him was bigger and better than other kids. At Waukegan High School in Illinois he was all-state in both football and basketball. He never tooted his own horn, although he could have. In high school music competitions he ranked first in the state on the French horn. There's an explanation for everything, of course. Both of his parents were music teachers. He also played the piano, violin and cornet. He could have played most major parts of "Rhapsody in Blue" by himself.

Although he went to Northwestern on a basketball scholarship, he actually went there to study music. When football coach Pappy Waldorf saw him throwing a football around in an intramural game, George Gershwin got shoved aside. Otto went on to become the Big Ten's MVP in both football and basketball in the same school year. In the spring of 1943 he had the third-highest batting average on the baseball team and in the fall he finished third in the Heisman Trophy voting.

He was also in the Navy's flight program and in 1944 he was transferred first to a Navy training center at Colgate University, where he played basketball, and then to North Carolina, where he played football for Bear Bryant. The Navy taught him to fly and Bear Bryant taught him the T formation.

When World War II ended, the Detroit Lions picked him in the first round of the National Football League draft, but Otto chose to sign with Paul Brown and the Cleveland Browns in the new All-America Football Conference. Since the AAFC did not start until 1946, Otto had a year to kill, which he used to play pro basketball with the Rochester Royals. The Royals won the championship in the National Basketball League.

So, let's see. The pro basketball championship in 1946 began a streak of six straight professional championships and 11 straight championship game appearances that lasted a decade from 1946 through 1955.

For 10 years he was the greatest quarterback in pro football, and the Browns were the greatest dynasty the game has ever known. The New England Patriots are good. So were the 49ers and the Packers and the Cowboys. I'm not saying we should dismiss them. I am saying that people forget how good the Browns were because their legacy has been tainted in recent decades by the "new Browns."

Graham pre-dated today's era of self-aggrandizement, choreographed dancing, body artwork, piercings, secret handshakes, selfies, entourages, bodyguards, guns, disposable housemates, private jets, charter flights, drugs, steroids and rehab.

Graham was part of the culture that actually believed sports heroes were role models.

Russ Carson, a retired vice-president from Penton Publishing, recalls riding home to Bay Village from Browns games in the back of Graham's station wagon in the early 1950s.

"We were in grade school in Bay Village," Carson said. "We would take the bus down to the Stadium and buy cheap tickets. Afterward we would hang around the locker-room door. The security guard was a big fat retired Cleveland policeman or at least one getting ready to retire. He didn't bother us. Eventually Otto came out and his wife would pull up in a Ford station wagon. A Ford. Not an expensive fancy car. We would pile in the back of the station wagon. He lived in western Bay Village. He would drive the length of Wolf Road through Bay Village. He'd slow down and drop us off at our street. After a while he'd remember some of our names and our streets. He sort of enjoyed this, as though he was doing his school bus service."

Carson remembers some of the conversations between Otto and his wife, Beverly. One Sunday the Browns mauled Washington quarterback Eddie LeBaron. On the ride home Otto suggested to Beverly that she call LeBaron's wife the next day and inquire about him.

"Even the superstars were normal in those days," added Carson. "It was a simpler, wonderful age. I'm glad we grew up at that time."

Mike Holland was in grade school in Lakewood at that time. Now a financial mogul in New York, he emailed me this account of his "Otto Graham Moment."

"In the autumn of 1953 I was on a kids' football team that was truly sandlot. I was too young for the St. Luke's CYO team. We were a ragtag group who played a number of other local ragtag teams. At the end of the season the team voted me the MVP, probably because I was the quarterback. Someone audaciously put a call in to Otto Graham to ask him to present the trophy at our team end of the season lunch in the 'projects' in Lakewood. Surprisingly, he said yes. He actually showed up.

"And I remember a large bandage on his forehead as a result of a cheap shot he had taken in that Sunday's game. (There had been a picture in The Plain Dealer sports section that Monday of him sitting on the field with his face covered in blood.) He was incredibly kind and unassuming. Except for the 20 kids and parents in the coach's modest home, nobody knew he had ever done such a wonderful thing.

"Decades later I saw him being interviewed on TV. He had some serious health problems. I found his address in Florida and sent a letter to tell him what an effect his generosity to some unknown kids had. He responded with a very gracious note. He passed away not long after. A true champion."

Maybe someone will check back on Johnny Manziel in a few years to see how it all turned out. It won't be me.

Touch of Color

WHEN THE ALL-AMERICA FOOTBALL Conference was formed in 1946 with eight teams located in cities from coast to coast, including Cleveland, the Cleveland Browns owner Arthur B. "Mickey" McBride earned the enmity of the other owners from the outset.

Bob Gries, whose father owned a small piece of that team, about 5 percent, recalls his father telling this story.

The original Browns included two black players, Marion Motley and Bill Willis, which some of the other owners found objectionable. This came up at an owners' meeting in Chicago. What they envisioned was a brand new league which would be an all-white league.

"Mickey was a stubborn Irishman and he would have none of it," Gries wrote in his family history, a hard-bound tome called "Five Generations—175 Years of Love for Cleveland."

Gries loosely quoted McBride as retorting, "We are going to play Motley and Willis and if you don't like it, I'll tell you what you can do with your team."

No doubt that is a sanitized version of the conversation. McBride was a street fighter from Chicago when he was brought to Cleveland to bust some heads and sort out the newspaper circulation war in the '30s. After finishing that job he became a taxi-cab tycoon.

McBride had no concept of white players or black players. As a matter of fact, he knew little about football, period. In his early days as an owner he relied for counsel on his son, Artie, who had absorbed some football knowledge as a student at Notre Dame. After hiring Paul Brown as his coach, on the advice of Artie, McBride stepped back and got out of the way. After all,

Paul Brown, who had coached Ohio State to the national championship in 1942, was the single biggest name in the new league.

Brown put together his first team essentially with players he coached or coached against in high school at Massillon, in college at Ohio State or in the U. S. Navy at Great Lakes Naval Training Station. Motley played high school ball at Canton McKinley, where his teams tangled with Brown's Massillon teams in the late '30s. Willis played for Brown on Ohio State's national championship team of 1942 and later on Brown's navy team at Great Lakes.

They were worth fighting for. Both Motley and Willis were inducted into the Pro Football Hall of Fame.

It would be nice to say that in 1946 the Cleveland Browns broke the color barrier in pro football, but that wasn't the case. That same year in the National Football League the Los Angeles Rams, which had just moved from Cleveland, were bullied into integrating by the Los Angeles Coliseum Commission. According to the terms of their lease, if the Rams refused to hire black players, they were not welcome in the Coliseum. Therefore, in 1946 the Rams signed Kenny Washington and Woody Strode, two players who had been stars at UCLA. Their college teammate was—get ready for this—Jackie Robinson, the baseball pioneer who also played college football.

The following year the Browns added black punter Horace Gillom, who had played for Paul Brown at Massillon. That same year five more teams in the AAFC followed the Browns' lead and signed black players. Another year later the Detroit Lions of the National Football League signed a black player.

The last holdout was the infamous George Preston Marshall, owner of the Washington Redskins, who once said, "We'll start signing Negroes when the Harlem Globetrotters start signing whites."

As in the earlier Los Angeles Rams case, Marshall was forced to integrate when his DC Stadium landlord hit him over the head with a sledgehammer. Stewart Udall, who was Secretary of the Interior, held up the Stadium lease to the bright light and threatened to evict the Redskins from the stadium that was federally owned.

As a famous philosopher once said, "When you have them by the gonads, their hearts and minds will follow."

As a result, the color barrier in Washington was broken in 1962 by Bobby Mitchell, whom the Browns had just traded in exchange for the rights to number one draft choice Ernie Davis. Marshall was forced to make the trade when Davis insisted he would never play for the Redskins. Davis never played for the Browns, either, because of a cruelly ironic twist of fate. Davis contracted leukemia and died within two years. Mitchell, however, went into the Hall of Fame.

Actually, when you talk about the color barrier in pro football, it was something that came and went. It wasn't like the Great Wall of China. As far back as 1904 the Shelby Steamfitters of the Ohio League paid a black player named Charles Follis.

In 1920, the first year of the NFL, two black players were gainfully employed. They were Fritz Pollard and Bobby Marshall. As a matter of fact, the next year Pollard became the first black head coach. From 1928 through 1933 five more black players entered the league for short periods of time.

Today almost 70 percent of the players in the NFL are black.

Bursting the Bubble

ACCORDING TO THE STORY, the All-America Football Conference folded after four seasons because the Browns totally dominated it. The Browns won every championship from 1946 through 1949 and nobody else had a chance. The team Paul Brown put together was head and shoulders above the competition. So the league evaporated. The National Football League absorbed three teams—Cleveland, Baltimore and San Francisco—and the remaining teams went defunct. Paul Brown, the smartest man in the room, was responsible. It seemed logical and for 65 years we swallowed it in one huge gulp.

"It's not true," said Bob Gries, whose family owned a piece of every pro football team in Cleveland for half a century. "The Browns didn't put the All-America Football Conference out of business. The Internal Revenue Service did."

Gries recalled the IRS's "Hobby Loss" rule, which asserted that an investor could deduct "hobby" losses against regular income from other businesses for only four years. In those days, pro football definitely was a hobby, and an affordable one as long as the IRS was an equal partner. Although investors were losing money, the losses reduced their income taxes, plus they enjoyed the privileges of ownership. In those days, by the way, the highest tax bracket was 91 percent. Oh, they could continue to lose money, but beyond four years they could not deduct the losses.

In 1949, after four years of no profits, the privileges expired and the AAFC went to the end zone in the sky, following so many other startup pro football leagues.

"Nobody was making money in pro football," Gries said.

This wasn't a phenomenon of the post-war period, it was the

nature of pro football from its beginning in 1920 until the 1960s when the first big national television contract kicked in.

For example, Cleveland was in and out of the NFL several times from 1920 until Gries' father made his first football investment in 1936 as a civic gesture.

"My father and 12 other men were original investors in the Cleveland Rams in 1936," Gries said. "They wanted Cleveland to be represented in this brand new eight-team league called the American Football League. They raised $10,000 for a franchise license and $25,000 in additional cash. Every Monday my father hosted the investors for lunch at the May Co. They added up what they owed the players that week, maybe $25 for this player, $50 for that player, maybe $100 for some, plus a laundry bill and coach's salary. Each man kicked in money to pay the week's expenses."

After one year in the American Football League, not to be confused with the All-America Football Conference of the 1940s, the Rams moved into the NFL. From an economic standpoint, nothing changed. The owners still met for lunch on Mondays and dug deep into their pockets to pay salaries and laundry bills.

The Rams survived the Great Depression and in 1941 the original investors sold the team to a pair of New York dandies named Dan Reeves and Fred Levy. The Cleveland football teams Reeves bought were polar opposites of the Broadway showgirls he fancied. They had three winning seasons in the 1920s—1923, '24 and '27—and didn't have another winning season until 1945 when they hit the jackpot. The Rams won the 1945 NFL championship, beating the Washington Redskins, 15-14, before 32,178 spectators on a frigid Sunday at Cleveland Municipal Stadium. The winning players' share was $1,469 for the Rams. The losing Redskins players got a runner-up bonus of $902. It was the kind of money the boys raised regularly at lunch at the huge May Co. department store, which, incidentally, the Gries family owned.

Having finally won a championship, Reeves packed up his Rams team and moved them to Los Angeles, which was more compatible with his lifestyle, leaving Cleveland alone with its new team, the fledgling Browns in the new All-America Football Conference. The year was 1946 and the IRS clock was ticking.

No Betting in the Press Box

THAT'S ONE OF MY prime rules of sportswriting. Never bet on a game you're covering. When your money is at stake, you will go insane trying to separate your reporting from your bookkeeping. Asked once whom he's rooting for in a big game, the great Los Angeles sportswriter Jim Murray said, "I'm rooting for the story." Great games make great stories. Be content with that.

I violated that rule once. It was an expensive lesson.

The Browns were in Atlanta to play the Falcons on a rainy Sunday afternoon, Oct. 17, 1976, and it looked like easy money. On Monday of that week the Falcons had fired their coach, Marion Campbell, and replaced him with a fellow named Pat Peppler. The circumstances were textbook. The Falcons were not very good. They were a 1966 expansion team and 10 years later still were looking for their first winning season. No one should have been surprised when Campbell was fired, but some members of the coaching staff were outraged. Three assistant coaches immediately quit in protest, including Bill Nelsen, who had been the Browns quarterback a few years earlier.

On Saturday night Nelsen stopped by the hotel to visit some old Browns teammates. As the night progressed the players drifted away and he found himself in the bar with his old newspaper and radio friends. No one was more comfortable in that situation than Bill Nelsen. We settled in.

Nelsen told us that the Falcons were in turmoil—the head coach fired, three assistants gone, a 1-4 record on the way to another dismal 4-10 mark, only 33,464 tickets sold for that week's game. When it came to the Falcons, the entire city of Atlanta was lethargic. This was classic inside information.

About midnight I went up to my room and called the well-known Irish gambler, Junior O'Malley, who had just arrived home from a night of revelry at Cavoli's Restaurant at West 116th Street and Clifton Boulevard. Every Saturday night, Junior and his ever-suffering wife Didi would rush home from Thistledown Racetrack and regale the patrons in Cavoli's with tales of triumph or heartbreak from that day's racing program. Junior always believed his next winner was only six furlongs away.

"Junior," I said, "can you get a bet down on the Browns game for me?"

Of course, he could. Junior specialized in horse racing but his people handled action on anyone or anything. Later, when his wife suffered a serious heart attack, Junior made a deal with God that he would not bet a horse for one year if she survived. Didi made it and Junior fulfilled his pledge. That's when he started betting football.

"The line is four. Browns favored by four. I want to bet $500 on the Browns to cover four," I said.

It was Junior who introduced me to horse racing, but this was the first time I had ever asked him to make a football bet for me. This was no two-dollar bet on the daily double. Five hundred bucks was a week's pay at The Plain Dealer.

"If you lose, you owe $550," Junior said, reminding me that the loser pays the 10 percent vigorish, or bookie's commission.

The Browns were a lock to cover four points. Besides Atlanta's problems, the Browns were trending up. They had defeated the Steelers the previous week. Brian Sipe was in the process of taking the quarterback's job away from Mike Phipps, who had been sidelined with a shoulder separation.

Sunday morning was overcast, gloomy and wet. I was bouncing on the balls of my feet. On the short bus ride to Fulton County Stadium, Browns beat reporter Chuck Heaton was smiling and relaxed. Radio announcer Gib Shanley looked supremely satisfied. I knew Gib. I knew he also jumped all over that four-point spread.

By halftime nobody was smiling. In the press box snack room

Gib looked like his dog just died. Somebody forgot to tell the Falcons to roll over and play dead.

Late in the fourth quarter the Browns clung to a three-point lead, 20-17, but they had driven deep into Atlanta territory. They were comfortably within field-goal range and kicker Don Cockroft was lined up to provide the crucial points I needed to cover. Mike Phipps had come off the injured list for the first time in a month to hold for extra points and field goals. Thank God. I was rescued from the brink of disaster.

The snap was good but suddenly all hell broke loose. Phipps fumbled the snap and Cockroft never got the kick off. The ball went over to the Falcons and I just lost $550. I then turned vengeful. I wanted Atlanta to march the length of the field and actually beat the Browns, which they almost did. Thom Darden's interception in the closing seconds preserved the Browns win.

It was a good Cleveland story but I could enjoy none of it. Darden was a last-minute hero as the Browns won their second in a row to even their record at 3-3. Greg Pruitt had a sensational day in the mud, rushing for 191 yards on 26 carries. What a great sidebar story Pruitt made, player of the game, the best rushing performance in the NFL that day. Sipe had a decent game passing. He was 12 of 18 for 134 yards. Despite the dark sky and the rain, the sun was shining on the Browns.

I gathered my quotes in the locker room and typed my sidebar stories like a robot. To this day, all I remember is Phipps fumbling the ball. In the locker room I got a comment from him on the fumble and I actually wanted to put my hands around his neck and strangle him. I had to look up all that other stuff in my files.

Gib Shanley tucked his rosters and stats in his briefcase and left the broadcast booth wearing a raincoat and a scowl. His disposition told me he lost more than a week's pay.

You're probably thinking the same thing I did. When something is too good to be true, it probably is.

Saul Silberman Played
Every Game

THE BROWNS HAVEN'T HAD a big playmaker in 20 years, but for 50 years before that they had a plethora of them. To name just a few, Otto Graham, Jim Brown, Frank Ryan, Bill Nelsen, Leroy Kelly, Brian Sipe, Greg Pruitt and Bernie Kosar come to mind. A true Browns fan could name another 10 without straining his cerebellum and another 10 after that.

But you wouldn't name Saul Silberman, the biggest playmaker of them all. In the early 1950s Saul made a big play on every Browns game. Not in the game. On the game.

Saul was a Clevelander whose first love was horse racing. He owned Randall Park, which sat on a parcel of land across the street from Thistledown Racetrack, and he also owned Tropical Park racetrack in Miami, Florida. And from 1953 to 1955 he owned half of the Browns.

Browns coach Paul Brown considered Saul a very loyal and interested owner.

"He called every week to see if we had any injuries," Brown said once.

History reminds us that horse racing and pro football were not exactly strangers to each other. A man named Homer Marshman, who owned harness racing tracks around Cleveland, also owned a good piece of the Cleveland Rams in the 1930s. In fact, they were named the Rams because Marshman had a soft spot in his heart for the Fordham University football team, which was known as the Rams. Marshman was an enthusiastic sportsman. He was in and out of pro football in Cleveland and by the late 1950s he owned 15 percent of the Browns.

As a side story, Art Rooney himself had a healthy respect for the sport of kings and, according to legend, acquired ownership of the Pittsburgh Steelers in the 1930s as payment of a gambling debt.

But, let us return to Mr. Silberman. When Browns founder Mickey McBride decided to take his profit and sell the Browns in 1953, the new owners were a group of prominent Cleveland businessmen that bought 50 percent. They included Herb Evans of Nationwide Insurance, Bob Gries of Morgan Steel, coach Paul Brown, Homer Marshman, Dave Jones and Ellis Ryan. The other 50 percent was purchased by Silberman and his friend Ralph DeChiaro of Miami. Needless to say, they were kindred spirits in the horse racing business.

None, however, was a more committed owner than Silberman.

"I never knew why he was so interested in the health of our team," Brown once remarked to another part-owner.

It certainly seemed like a laudable trait until NFL commissioner Bert Bell came calling one day in 1955 and issued an ultimatum.

"Get rid of Silberman," the commissioner said to the owners who were not connected to Silberman.

The reason became clear. Silberman was gambling heavily on Browns games. The commissioner demanded that they buy out Silberman's half-interest in the team or he would revoke the Browns' franchise. There was no hint of game-fixing, of course. Paul Brown would have sniffed that out. Nevertheless, it was clear that the NFL finally was going upscale.

The other partners acted quickly and purchased Silberman's half-interest in the team for $600,000, which seemed to establish the value of the Browns at $1.2 million, a staggering sum. Two years earlier Silberman and his pal had bought the same half for $300,000. Pro football's meteoric ride was just beginning.

Great Impersonators

WHEN NEV CHANDLER WALKED into a room, he drew a crowd. He was immediately surrounded. Such was the magnetism of his personality. Everyone wanted to be near him. Nev, who was the main sports anchor at WEWS-TV (Channel 5), was also a compulsive comedian and mimic.

For example, Nev's impression of John Cooper sounded more like the old Ohio State coach than the real John Cooper. One night Nev was a guest on a local sports call-in radio show and when a listener asked a question about Ohio State football, Nev instinctively went into his Cooper voice.

"I want to get the tight end more involved in our offense," Nev said and then he elaborated. Nev could elaborate like nobody in town. He was the great elaborator.

A few minutes later the real John Cooper was on the radio with his Ohio State Football Coach's Show on a state-wide radio network.

"I just heard you on another station saying you wanted to get the tight end more involved in your offense," said a caller.

"I was on another station?" said a puzzled Cooper who then wisely moved on. "I don't remember saying that, but, yes, I would like to get the tight end more involved in our offense."

Cooper then elaborated.

Nev was a natural. He also mastered Browns coach Sam Rutigliano, the insufferable Howard Cosell, and Rico Carty, the Indians "Big Mon" who was a general in the Dominican army.

There was a time when everybody did impressions of Mudcat Grant, the charming old pitcher who was one of the Indians' television announcers. Mudcat, who brought quaint colloquialisms from his native Florida into the broadcast booth, probably was best-known for introducing the expression "chin music" to Cleveland baseball fans.

Mudcat was so beloved that entire conversations were conducted in his dialect. Not surprisingly, Nev was the best but other people, such as Dino Lucarelli, the Indians' public relations chief, were close. Frequently, Nev used his Mudcat voice when he called Dino and Dino responded in the same voice.

"Dino is really getting good at this," Nev thought to himself during one of those calls. He was getting too good, in fact.

"Who be this?" Nev finally asked.

"This be Mud," said the real Mudcat, who happened to be sitting in Dino's office and answered the phone because Dino had stepped away.

"Who be this?" Mud asked.

"Gib Shanley," Nev said quickly and hung up.

Tom Bush, a radio and television personality from the 1970s, '80s and '90s, appeared in many Big Chuck and Little John skits on Fox 8, but he became famous for one voice—Bob Feller.

During one game against the Yankees at the old Stadium, a writer leaned up to Bush in the press box and said, "Do Feller." Bush loved requests. It meant that at least one person was actually listening. So he went into a Bob Feller monolog about opening a K Mart in Iowa, whereupon the Yankee public relations man, Bob Fishel, recognized the voice and popped up.

"I swear," said Bush, "he looked right at me and said, 'Bob!'"

Many years earlier Fishel worked for the Indians and spent much time with Feller. Bush certainly didn't look like Feller, but several years had passed and Fishel momentarily was fooled.

Bush tormented the Indians' front-office employees and his own radio stations with bizarre phone calls.

"The real Bob Feller called the radio station, but the board operator wouldn't put him through. The board operator thought it was me," Bush said.

After Feller died, Bush called Indians PR man Bob DiBiasio and left this message on his voice mail: "This is Bob Feller. I'm calling from heaven. I just ran into Ted Williams. Funny thing. He had no head. But he's still hitting .320."

When it came to sustained dialectic brilliance, however, no one approached a man who called himself "The Predickher" on Gary Dee's WHK radio show in the late 1970s and early '80s.

You probably think that anybody who would call Gary Dee was a total moron, but the Predickher actually held a master's degree from an accredited university. I have known him for 40 years but for some reason he made me pledge not to reveal his true identity. The secrecy makes no sense. Most of those who may have wanted to kill him those many years ago are themselves dead. But the Predickher never forgot that someone set fire to Gary's beloved boat and burned it to the waterline. So, I must protect his privacy. It was a deal-breaker.

He was a white guy living in a bachelor cottage in Rocky River overlooking the Cleveland Yacht Club. Here's the Predickher's story.

"It was a Monday morning and I was laying in bed listening to Gary Dee on the radio," the Predickher began. "Dee went off on a rant. He was reading the front page of The Plain Dealer, a story about the skyrocketing unemployment rate in the black community. He asked for black men to call and explain why they don't work. Nobody called. He kept asking. Not a call.

"I'm laying there and I guess I got tired of the silence. I called and told him I was a black man and I didn't work because I didn't have to work. I had the Bengals minus three, the Raiders plus three and the Browns minus six. I won $3,000. Why should I work? I used all black lingo."

"Are you really black?" Dee asked. "Pronounce the word, ask."

"Axe," said the Predickher who was born with a gift for dialects.

Dee swallowed the bait in one gulp.

"What are you, some kind of predictor?" Dee asked.

"Yes, I am the Predickher," said the Predickher.

From that moment, the Predickher became a staple of Gary Dee's Friday morning show, spouting betting advice on college and pro football for several seasons. If his call was a minute late, Dee would say, "He's probably in jail again."

In real life the Predickher actually was a highly-regarded football handicapper named Will Cover (another pseudonym) with real-life clients who paid handsomely for his advice.

There were those who called the Dee show claiming to be the Predickher, but there were holes in their dialects.

"You're not the Predickher," Dee would snarl.

"They're imposteriors," the Predickher said.

One fateful week the Predickher released his famous pick on the Penn State-Alabama game. He picked the favorite, Penn State, to beat Alabama and cover four points.

"Jerry, if I'm wrong," the Predickher promised, "I will assassinate myself on the air."

He always called him Jerry, not Gary.

Alabama upset Penn State with a disputed touchdown pass in the waning minutes. The Predickher was humiliated. The next week, as advertised, the Predickher said goodbye to "Jerry" and the radio audience. He lit the fuse on a M-80 firecracker, tossed it into his back yard and held the phone toward it. On the radio the blast sounded like a gunshot.

"He was a man of his word," said Dee.

For a year the Predickher was silent, which wasn't unusual for a dead guy. Dee, meanwhile, continued to taunt blacks and whites, trying to start a race war on the radio, all for the sake of a rating point or two. But Friday mornings didn't have the same pizzazz, until Dee got a call from a man saying he was an orderly at the Cleveland Clinic. The orderly said he went into a mysterious room that was cordoned off behind a door that said, "No Admittance," where he found a body on a gurney. The body was that of the Predickher, who had just undergone a brain transplant. The orderly said that a Dr. White had transplanted the brain of a baboon into the cranium of the Predickher, who soon afterward returned to the Gary Dee show. It made a wonderful story.

"Jerry, I don't know what happened," the Predickher told Dee, "but I've been climbing a lot of trees and eating a lot of bananas."

WHK fired Gary Dee in September 1983, while he was on vacation. He bounced around, never staying long, at radio stations in New York, Washington, Los Angeles and back in Cleveland at WWWE. His health deteriorated and he died on Nov. 10, 1995, at the age of 60.

The Predickher attended the funeral service at the Grdina-Faulhaber Funeral Home on Lake Shore Boulevard on Cleveland's East Side.

"I didn't know what to expect," said the Predickher. "I said there would either be 300 people there or 30."

The Predickher was close. He says there were 20. Liz Richards, the fourth of Gary's five wives, was there. The Predickher expressed his condolences to one of Gary's sons, who said the stress of five wives led to Gary's declining health.

"How did you know my dad?" said the son.

"I was the Predickher," he said.

Gary's son embraced him like a long-lost brother. "My dad would be so proud," he said.

The Predickher sat down on a folding chair and waited for the service to begin. George Forbes, at one time the most dynamic black politician in Cleveland who had deftly played off Gary for fun and profit, came in and sat down next to the Predickher. They introduced themselves.

"How did you know Gary?" said Forbes.

"I was the Predickher," he said.

Forbes looked at the white guy from Rocky River, threw his arms in the air and almost had a heart attack.

By the way, the Grdina-Faulhaber Funeral Home is now the

Calhoun Funeral Home, serving a black clientele almost exclusively. I'm sure the race-baiting shock jock appreciates the irony.

Meanwhile, the Predickher is in good health. He gambles, drinks and drives around in a Mercedes-Benz convertible. He never married.

Rumors of My Death

THAT'S ONE OF THE most quotable lines attributed to Mark Twain. Responding to a report that he had passed away, the revered American writer and humorist sent a telegram to the Associated Press saying, "Rumors of my death are greatly exaggerated."

So it was with Edward J. DeBartolo, the owner of Thistledown Racetrack, when James J. "Junior" O'Malley called me from Hot Springs, Arkansas, on New Year's Day of 1974.

Junior was the most degenerate gambler I ever knew. Usually he confined his wagering to the racetrack. He worked at Thistledown as a mutuel clerk, punching out win, place and show tickets to hopeful horse players, but mostly he punched out tickets for himself. In the winter when the racetrack was closed Junior worked as a proof-reader at The Plain Dealer. It was a well-paying union job and Junior hated it. Every spring he took a leave of absence from the paper and returned to Thistledown for half the pay.

On this particular winter's day, Junior had taken a break from the newspaper composing room and was in Arkansas, where he knew a trainer who had taken a string of fresh ponies to Oaklawn Park. As usual Junior was poking around the barns when he picked up a fresh rumor. It was more of a question. Could Junior confirm a report that Thistledown owner Edward DeBartolo had died?

Junior tracked me down in the sports department about dinner time. The easiest way to confirm DeBartolo's status was to call him. If he answered the phone I would say, "Happy New Year," and ask him how he was feeling. If he sounded reasonably well, I would relay that information to Junior.

However, I did not have DeBartolo's home phone number and he wasn't listed in the directory. His corporate office in Youngstown was closed for the holiday and his racetrack offices were closed for the season. Usually I would call the Thistledown publicity man, Paul Wilcox, but he and his wife were off on a cruise.

The question of DeBartolo's health transcended mere curiosity. If he had indeed departed this mortal coil, it was a headline story. It was a "Stop the presses!" story. DeBartolo was one of the richest men in America. He built and owned hundreds of shopping malls all over the United States. At one time he owned 10 percent of the malls in the country. He was on Forbes Magazine's list of the wealthiest men in America as his net worth approached one billion dollars. This was in the 1970s, when a billion really was a billion.

Thistledown was only a hobby, however. He often took a private plane from his Youngstown office to the racetrack. The pilot actually landed in the infield at Thistledown and parked the single-engine plane behind the toteboard. Everybody would see his plane land and the employees would snap to attention.

In the early 1970s he revealed to me his interest in buying the Cleveland Indians baseball team from Vernon Stouffer. I wrote that story in The Plain Dealer in the morning, and that afternoon Bob August in the Cleveland Press wrote a critical column about DeBartolo's second-rate race track and questioned his credentials to own a baseball team.

"The hell with this," DeBartolo snarled. "He wants to run me out of baseball before I even get in it. Baseball can forget about me."

DeBartolo went on to buy two more race tracks, Louisiana Downs in Shreveport and Remington in Oklahoma. He also bought two professional sports teams—the San Francisco 49ers football team, which he turned over to his son, and the Pittsburgh Penguins hockey team, which he presented to his daughter.

If Edward J. DeBartolo had died, it would have been the lead story on page one of The Plain Dealer the next day and the story would have been played prominently on the financial pages of every major newspaper in the country. It is not the type of tip you expect to hear from a thoroughbred horse trainer up to his ankles in Arkansas horse manure, but in the newspaper business you can't dismiss anybody. Anytime the phone rings it might be the biggest story of your life. It was my job to check it out and I had a plan. I smiled to myself. Damn, I was smart. I was one damn smart reporter.

A friend of mine once made an accidental blunder when he prematurely put a former Indians manager in his grave. While writing a nostalgia piece about an Indians player from the 1930s, Plain Dealer sportswriter Dennis Lustig mentioned the player's manager, the late Roger Peckinpaugh.

The next day I answered a ringing phone in the sports department.

"May I speak to Dennis Lustig?" the caller said.

"Sure. Who's calling?" I replied.

"This is the 'late' Roger Peckinpaugh," said Roger Peckinpaugh, who still lived in Shaker Heights and read The Plain Dealer every morning.

I never forgot that. It's never a good policy to bury people while they're still breathing unless you are mentally near death yourself. As I said, I had a plan.

There should be two books on every reporter's desk—the phone book and a dictionary. Of the two, the phone book is the reporter's best friend. Sadly, the name you need never seems to be there anymore. People cancel land lines today and use only cell phones, which are not listed in the phone book.

But in 1974 the Youngstown Yellow Pages held the answer. The Plain Dealer had phone books from almost every city in Ohio. I grabbed the Youngstown directory, flipped open the Yellow Pages and turned to "Funeral Directors." Two of them had Italian names. If DeBartolo died, one of them would know it. People who remain closely associated with their ethnic heritage are particularly clannish when they die. Irish are buried by Irish, Poles by Poles, Jews by Jews, Protestants by Protestants and Italians by Italians. I called both Italian funeral homes, one at a time. A live person answers the phone 24 hours a day at funeral homes.

"I'm calling from the Cleveland Plain Dealer," I said. "Do you have Mister DeBartolo?"

There was a pause.

"Do you mean Edward DeBartolo?"

"Yes."

"No, we don't have him."

"Thank you. Goodbye."

The exchange was repeated virtually verbatim with the second funeral home and the answer was the same. If the only two Italian funeral homes in Youngstown didn't have his body, Edward DeBartolo was alive. I called Junior O'Malley in Arkansas and told him. End of story. I left the paper and watched the end of the Orange Bowl game on television at a bar on East Ninth Street. Penn State beat LSU, 16-9.

The next day I sashayed into The Plain Dealer sports department and all hell was breaking loose. The usually mild-mannered Edward DeBartolo was on the phone and he was running a temperature. Our sports editor, Hal Lebovitz, handed me the phone.

"What the hell is going on?" DeBartolo demanded. "Banks from Boston to San Francisco are in a panic."

DeBartolo was an anachronism, a one-man operation. He had mortgages in dozens of banks from coast to coast. In fact, he owned three banks in Florida. When banks did business with the DeBartolo Corporation, they did business directly with Edward J. If he were to die suddenly, the bankers had the heart attacks.

In retrospect, it's easy to rationalize what happened. A phone call from The Plain Dealer was as good as a death certificate. I should have explained myself. I left each funeral home thinking the other had the body of one of the most important financiers in America and they spread the word. In 12 hours the word went from Mahoning County east and west over four time zones.

"Why didn't you call me at home?" DeBartolo said. "I was at home watching the Orange Bowl game. I had 500 dollars bet on it."

"I didn't have your phone number," I replied lamely.

That never happened again. We exchanged personal phone numbers and later that year, when he was working on a deal to buy a racetrack in Tampa, he returned my call from his private jet plane. He was 35,000 feet above North Carolina. I could hear his breathing in the light air.

DeBartolo died on Dec. 19, 1994, at the age of 85. I read about it in the New York Times.

Jim Fixx the Running Man

IN THE EARLY '70S I went on a diet and took up running. I reduced my beer intake from six beers a day to six a week. Before long I was logging three miles in 18 minutes every day, which was considered a very good time for a casual runner. The pounds melted away. I was 36 and was getting into good shape.

One hot summer afternoon, while I was chugging around the track at Finnie Stadium in Berea, where the Baldwin-Wallace College football team played and where the Browns maintained their full-time practice facilities, the Browns' trainer Leo Murphy ran out of the locker room and made a bee line toward me.

"How long did it take for you to get out of shape?" Leo demanded.

"You know me, Leo," I said. "I've spent my life trying to get out of shape."

"Well, you're not gonna get back in shape in a day," said Leo. "Are you trying to give yourself a heart attack?"

A heart attack! No, I didn't want a heart attack. So I quit running. Just like that. I went home, took a deep drag on a Pall Mall, cleared an entire shelf in the refrigerator for beer and never ran again. That was four decades ago.

About the same time, a fellow named Jim Fixx was running straight into a heart attack.

Neil Zurcher, Fox 8's "One Tank Trips" man and one of the best storytellers ever on television, knew Fixx back in the 1950s, when Fixx was attending Oberlin College. Fixx landed a part-time job as a cub reporter on the Oberlin News-Tribune, the weekly paper, where Zurcher also worked.

Zurcher remembers Fixx as a typical aspiring young newspaperman. He made $25 a week, which kept him in beer and cigarettes. It wasn't much money, but it was a small fortune to Fixx, whose father, a copy editor at Time Magazine, had died of a heart attack at the age of 43 the year young Jim entered college.

What set Fixx apart from other beginning journalists was his IQ. It was through the roof. Fixx was a member of Mensa. Upon graduating from Oberlin College, he began a succession of jobs. He worked at a small daily newspaper in Florida. He moved back to New York, where he grew up, and worked at several magazines including Saturday Review, McCall's and Life. He published three collections of puzzles for elitists: "Games for the Superintelligent," "More Games for the Superintelligent" and "Solve It."

He made a little money, but never enough. He was well into his 30s, he had a mortgage in Connecticut, four children, a wife and an ex-wife whom he paid $12,000 a year in alimony. He weighed 240 pounds, smoked two packs of cigarettes a day and felt like he was living life on a treadmill. He decided to take up jogging as therapy for a torn calf muscle.

He didn't establish a regular running schedule. He went for a jog when it occurred to him and when he felt motivated. What people in our business try to avoid are more deadlines. For Fixx, running became a habit, not a deadline. It was relaxing. He felt better. He drank less. He began losing weight. And then the entire plan backfired. He wound up on a deadline.

Looking around for a way to make a quick 10 grand to appease his ex-wife, he noticed an increasing number of joggers in Central Park and on the urban trails. He also noticed a growing number of newsstand magazines devoted to running. Surely, he thought, he could get a 10-grand advance on a book about running. He could whip it out in a few weeks. As he envisioned it, such a book would be breezy, superficial and easy to write. The sooner it was finished, the sooner he would get the advance. He picked up some magazines and skimmed a few books. That would suffice for research.

What he did not expect, however, is that he actually became interested in the subject and in the end it totally consumed him. Ten years later, he was 60 pounds lighter than when he began jogging, and Random House published his book—"The Complete Book of Running." Within two months it soared to number one on the New York Times' best-seller list and it stayed there for a year. He crisscrossed the country on a promotional tour, appearing on television in 25 cities. He was particularly impressed with Fred Griffith, who interviewed him on WEWS Channel 5 in Cleveland. This was 1977. Fixx was 45 years old and he was an instant millionaire. The first $12,000 went to his ex-wife. Then he went through a second divorce. He wrote out a much bigger check to ex-wife number two.

He wrote a second "complete book of running" and then he wrote a book called "Jackpot," sort of a diary of his big score. He was fabulously wealthy. He made millions and was set for life.

He continued to run and in 1984, at the age of 53, he fell over dead of a heart attack while jogging on Vermont Route 15 in Hardwick, Vermont. An autopsy revealed he had an enlarged heart and three clogged arteries—95 percent, 85 percent and 70 percent. He left behind four children, two comfortable ex-wives and a bulging bank account. A few days before he died a doctor friend on Cape Cod was worried about Jim's heart and advised him to slow down.

In Cleveland a newspaper reporter named Darrell Holland, who covered the religion beat for The Plain Dealer, took a similar path. In December 1980 life became a struggle. He was in El Salvador covering the murder of four Catholic missionaries, two of whom were from Cleveland—Ursuline nun Dorothy Kazel and lay missionary Jean Donovan. It was one of the biggest stories of the year and he ran out of cigarettes. It was difficult to find any in El Salvador. Like many of us on the paper at the time, he had smoked for years. Then his back started bothering him. He was in nicotine withdrawal and his back hurt in the middle of one of the biggest stories of his life.

He wrapped up his coverage and returned home with a bad back. He worked into spring, then checked into Lutheran Hospital's acclaimed spine unit where they put him in traction for three weeks. Darrell was headed for back surgery until he began working with a physical therapist who dissuaded him from surgery and at the same time persuaded him to quit smoking.

"I switched to cigars," he said. "Because I hated cigars I thought it would help me quit smoking, and it did."

He began walking his wife Ann's lap dog, Pudgie, at night. One night they were walking near the Bay Village High School track and the old reporter's Eureka moment struck him.

"I tied Pudgie to the fence and ran around the track," he said. "The next night I ran around twice. Third night three times, and after that I stopped counting."

In 1981 he ran his first 10k and in 1982 he ran his first marathon. He was 50 years old. Two years later he read in the paper that Jim Fixx had died. He had read both his books. He was a year younger than Fixx.

Darrell went on to run six marathons and compete in 12 triathlons, and then he took up mountain climbing. By the time he was 83 Darrell had climbed mountains all over the world, including Mount Everest.

"Not to the top, of course. But I reached the base camp at 18,500 feet," he said.

He has climbed Mount Kilimanjaro, Mount St. Helens and the Inca Trail in Peru. Back at home, Darrell walks, runs or rides his bike almost everywhere.

What does this mean? Fixx had all the money in the world and didn't live long enough to spend it. Holland, who worked at The Plain Dealer from 1974 until 1997, lives the high life on a reporter's pension.

"They can't understand why I do the things I do," Darrell said. "Every morning I run at least an hour."

Deep down, however, Darrell knows exactly why he does the things he does and Fixx couldn't.

"Three of my grandparents lived into their mid-80s, two almost to 90. Fixx's father died of a heart attack at age 43," Darrell said.

So he got a free pass. It's all genetics.

"I got lucky," he said.

Meanwhile, in the summer of 2015, I am still alive and have not run in 41 years except to catch a plane. Thank you, Leo Murphy, who also is still alive. Neither one of us, however, is presumptuous enough to buy any green bananas.

Last Resting Place

EVERYBODY THINKS ABOUT DYING or some derivative of the subject. For example, I had an old friend, the gambler Junior O'Malley, who was consumed with worry about the music at his funeral. He had many friends with fine voices who promised him they would do the singing, but one after another, they died. Ultimately, Junior sang at his own funeral. He recorded his favorite song into a little tape recorder and it was played as his casket was being wheeled down the center aisle of St. Rose's Church on Cleveland's West Side. The hilarious details of this story are documented in my first book, "Crazy, with the Papers to Prove It," which you are encouraged to pick up.

I would like to insert a personal story here. I have made a specific request that the Navy Hymn be played at my funeral as a final gesture of contempt for the Army. I was never in the Navy but I was in the Army.

As for eulogies, I have a cousin, John Coughlin, an old truant officer, who is acclaimed for his witty eulogies. No maudlin testimonials for him—or his subjects. I know people who attend the funeral Mass for people they don't even know when they learn that cousin John is the eulogist.

There is an old story, totally apocryphal, about the funeral for the most disliked man in a little Irish town. There was a surprisingly good turnout, mainly because everyone wanted to be sure he was dead. At end of the Mass, the priest asked the mourners—an ironic term in this case—who was going to speak on behalf of the deceased. No one moved. There was, literally, dead silence.

Finally, the priest said, "Then we'll sit here until somebody says something about this poor man."

At that, a man in the back of the church stood up and said,

"His brother was worse." The man then sat down after delivering the all-time briefest eulogy.

I have instructed my daughter, Mary, to do my eulogy and I gave her two guidelines. In the opening minutes of her talk, I want her to call on wonderful, humorous stories that render the mourners hysterical with laughter. At the end, however, I told her I want weeping and wailing. Touch on every human emotion. By the time they are putting my casket in the hearse, I want women to collapse with exhaustion and men to stumble blindly through their tears. I'll be watching.

Some people are very particular about their final resting place and right at the top of this list is Jerry McKenna, the world-renowned sculptor. He spent his high school years in Lakewood, did more than 20 years in the Air Force and now lives in San Antonio, where his studio is located. His heart, however, is at Notre Dame.

"I have a niche in the mausoleum at Notre Dame," he said. "My name is already on it and the year, 1937, along with the dash. All they have to do is add the year after the dash and I'm all set."

My old friend, Mickey Mishne, the auto race writer from The Plain Dealer, had his ashes scattered on the grounds of Watkins Glen in New York, where he spent many happy summer weekends covering the U.S. Grand Prix. This was not Mickey's idea, although I'm sure he was pleased. Mickey's brother, Ernie, made that call after Mickey was murdered by his wife's boyfriend.

The ashes of Eliot Ness, the famous "Untouchable," were scattered on a pond in Lakeview Cemetery because of his fondness for water.

I knew a sailing enthusiast from Lakewood who preferred that his ashes be scattered on Lake Erie. Accordingly, his friends sailed a mile out into the lake from Rocky River and as they tossed the ashes overboard, the wind changed and blew the ashes back into the boat. Luckily, the skipper was prepared for anything. He sucked up the ashes with a Dust Buster and tossed the entire Dust Buster into the lake.

Bob Hope was in his 90s the last time he visited Cleveland, and paid his respects to his parents who were buried at a cemetery on the East Side.

"This is such a peaceful spot," Hope said, noting the shady tree and the manicured grass. "This might be a good spot for me."

"But Bob," said his wife, "all our friends are in California."

"OK," said Bob. "Do what you want. Surprise me."

Nobody had a sweeter sendoff than Bill Baxter, an old baseball player from Chippewa Lake. Bill organized his first baseball team at the age of 12 and he was still playing organized softball into his early 70s.

"He was the biggest baseball fan I knew," recalled his grandson, Brandon Baxter, a one-time sports producer at Channel 8. "I listened to him tell stories about Lou Gehrig and Ted Williams."

Mr. Baxter's daughter, Gayle Foster, who wrote a nine-page pamphlet about her father, said they planned to bury his ashes at Mound Hill Cemetery in Seville.

"But then Mother remembered Dad saying he wanted to be buried on the pitcher's mound," said his daughter. "The Indians' new stadium at Gateway was nearing completion in 1994 and my husband was on the construction crew."

"Oh, no," said her husband. "Are you crazy? Those grounds are immaculate and security is extremely tight. But there are flower beds just outside the gates and maybe you could do it there."

And so, that's where Bill Baxter wound up. He died on Jan. 26, 1994, at the age of 75. His daughter held onto his ashes for two months and on Sunday, March 27, eight days before the 1994 home opener, the first official game played in the new Jacobs Field, the family went to services at United Methodist Church in Chippewa Lake and then headed downtown. They parked alongside Jacobs Field on Carnegie Avenue.

Before getting out of their van, they read an eulogy, said "The Lord's Prayer" and sang a hymn. Then they got out of the van and gathered around a strip of bare dirt near Gate D, the southwest corner of the ballpark. It was about 1 o'clock in the afternoon and the avenue was deserted. There were no pedestrians and no cars were in sight. Mr. Baxter's son, Bruce, who had his father's ashes hidden in a plastic bag up the sleeve of his coat, emptied them onto the patch of dirt outside Gate D.

"As soon as we finished what we're pretty certain is illegal, people started to appear all over the place," Mr. Baxter's daughter wrote in her pamphlet. "There was traffic on the street. Cars pulled up and people got out to explore the new ballpark. A security man with a walkie-talkie came along. No one said a word to us. It was really like God was watching out for us. We felt good about what we had done."

"Then we got out of there," said grandson Brandon. "It was cold, dreary and gray but there was no wind, so we weren't worried about my grandfather winding up on East 55th Street."

Eventually grass was planted on that little patch of dirt. It was hoped that when they turned over the earth to plant the grass, Mr. Baxter was permanently mixed into the landscape and helped grow the seeds.

When he died, old Bill Baxter still had a ball and glove in the trunk of his car in case anyone he encountered wanted to play catch. I wonder if there's a ghost playing catch on the corner of Ontario and Carnegie.

Married for His Money

IT ALL STARTED WHEN some guy sucker-punched Tony Alesci in a bar on the East Side back in 1975. Whoever that guy was, it was the dumbest thing he ever did. His life has been in danger from that moment.

Tony was a former catcher in the Chicago White Sox system. He came out of Maple Heights High School and Arizona State University with all the potential in the world. He planned it all. He would play in the major leagues, make a bundle of money and retire after about 15 years. Then he would take his money and open a restaurant with a fine bar.

There's an old saying: If you want to give God a good laugh, tell Him your plans. Well, back in the mid-1960s God was having a hilarious time with Tony Alesci. God converted him into a catcher who couldn't throw, which was quite a trick. He took Tony's rocket arm and turned it into a wet noodle. Tony spent more time in the doctor's office than on the ballfield and by 1969 he was finished. He reached Class AA and went no higher in the White Sox organization.

Tony would have been an ideal baseball hero. The fans would have loved him. He had the looks, he had the personality, he had the savoir faire. He also had a major-league thirst. He was a four-tool prospect.

It took him several years to forget that he was a ballplayer. He haunted the old Stadium, visiting with his old friends who did reach the big leagues. But by 1975 Tony grew up and found refuge in golf, boating and bars.

The night he was sucker-punched he was slaking a fine thirst after a round of golf. The police broke up the fight before Tony could deliver even one retaliatory blow, which is what really grieved him, because his nose was broken and his blood ruined a good Lacoste golf shirt. Tony could have resolved everything if the police had not been so quick to intervene, but in that joint a cop was on duty every night.

Tony, obviously, is Italian and you know what they say about Italians and their grudges. They take their grudges to their graves. That's why you'll always see at least six husky pall bearers carry an Italian to his final resting place. No skinny guys need apply. All those grudges are in there with them.

He returned to that bar every night for the next six months looking for his assailant and to this day he hasn't found him. But on the 180th night he did meet a young woman named Margaret Jaketic, who knocked his lights out without laying a glove on him.

He sent a round of drinks to her table. His Mediterranean charm was irresistible. After a few more drinks he invited her to go boating. His 24-foot Sea Ray was docked at the East 55th Street Marina. In a weak moment, she said yes.

"I flipped for this girl the moment she walked into the bar," Tony told me.

Here is proof that love is blind. The navigational opening in the breakwall must be half a mile wide, and Tony missed it.

"I hit the breakwall straight on at 40 miles an hour," he recalled. "There was a hole in the bow big enough for three men to crawl through. I figured we were going to sink. I put a life jacket on Margaret—I didn't even know her last name—and she was limp as a rag doll. I couldn't believe she was sleeping through all that. She happened to be unconscious. The crash had broken her neck.

"I didn't know how much time we had before the boat sank. I sent out a 'Mayday' on the boat's radio. The Coast Guard rescued us and took her to St. John's Hospital."

Margaret was in traction for six weeks. Over the course of the year she underwent a bone graft operation and had to wear an orthopedic collar.

It was a hell of a first date.

"I went to see her in the hospital every day," Tony said. "She told me to go away. She said she knew it was an accident but she couldn't stand to look at me. I was persistent. I learned her last name. She started to tolerate me. After a month she even started to like me."

Margaret didn't like him all that much. She sued him and collected a bundle from his insurance company, well into six figures before the string of zeroes bumped into a decimal point.

"Well," Tony said to himself, "Not only is this woman beautiful, now she is rich."

So he married her for his money. They had a baby and invested the insurance money in a restaurant called Meximilian's in Mentor which they ran for many years. They sold it only a few years ago and moved to Phoenix.

You know what God is saying.

"Tony, I owed you one."

Stealing the Davis Cup

WE WERE BLESSED WITH two great tennis promoters here in Cleveland, two men who brought us much joy and excitement.

The first was Jack Kramer, the world's number-one ranked player in the world before he became a promoter and organized the first professional tour in the early 1950s, and the second was Bob Malaga, who brought us international events in the 1960s and '70s.

Kramer, actually, was just a guy who passed through. He came to Cleveland once a year and stayed for a week. A tall Californian, Kramer was 26 and at the peak of his game when he won Wimbledon and Forest Hills in 1947. Seven years later he changed the game when he launched the first professional tour.

Until Kramer came along, tennis was purely amateur. The thought of actually offering prize money was anathema. But the time had come. Golf's pro tour had been around for decades. So, by 1954 Kramer signed up most of the leading players in the world, starting with Pancho Gonzales, the number one ranked player in the world from 1952 to 1960. Soon other top players turned pro, such as Pancho Segura, Lew Hoad, Ken Rosewall, Tony Trabert, Don Budge, Frank Sedgeman and Ken McGregor. The pro tour was quite a departure from traditional tennis, which was still purely amateur. The players who turned pro were excluded for many years from the most famous tournaments in the world, such as Wimbledon, Forest Hills, the Australian and French Opens. The pros were tainted not because money was involved but because money was out in the open. They were playing for prize money. For Gonzales, in particular, it was strictly business. He was a strange man—surly, friendless and rude. He was married six times and, according to Segura,

the nicest thing he ever said to any of his wives was, "Shut up."
He was, however, a brilliant player and people paid to see him.
He was a celebrity.

Starting in 1954 Cleveland was a regular stop on Kramer's pro
tour. Actually, the matches were played in Lakewood, at Lakewood Park located on the lake at Lake Avenue and Belle Avenue.
The amenities were simple—picnic areas, community swimming
pool and lighted tennis courts. It wasn't a dress-up affair. It was
on the West Side, for Pete's sake. As kids we pedaled our bikes
there. Clark Graebner, the future star who grew up in Lakewood
and went to Lakewood High School, was still in grade school
when he started to hang around the tennis matches. Chuck
Heaton, who also played tennis at Lakewood High School, was
an established football writer at The Plain Dealer, but he sometimes stopped by Kramer's tennis tournament and wrote a few
paragraphs about it. It was not headline news, but it was one of
the quaint things Lakewood had going.

Within a few years professional tennis became de rigueur
around the world and Kramer was gone from Lakewood Park,
onward and upward to bigger things.

In the 1960s downtown lawyer Bob Malaga surfaced and soon
his name became synonymous with tennis. When he stole the
Davis Cup from Forest Hills, New York, it was like purloining
the Mona Lisa from the Louvre. He got the world's attention.

Hell, back in the neighborhood he was already famous. Before
he finished high school at Cathedral Latin everybody in town
heard of the Slovak kid from Collinwood. He scored the first
touchdown and kicked the last extra point in the 1944 Charity
Game as Latin spanked Lincoln, 33-0, before 52,888 fans at the
old Stadium. A few months later the same two schools met for
the Senate basketball championship and Malaga again played a
starring role. His last-second basket tied the game and sent it
into overtime as Latin edged Lincoln, 34-32, at the old Cleveland Arena. In the spring of 1945 Malaga won the state tennis
championship.

From there it was off to Michigan State, where he lettered in tennis for four straight years and also played freshman football until a bad experience against Notre Dame ended that. Malaga was a defensive end playing special teams against the Fighting Irish freshmen.

"As an end," he said, "we're instructed on the kickoff to run down the field along the sideline and then cut in to make the tackle. At the cut I got hit by a couple of huge Irishmen and landed in the first row of the stadium. My next trip was to the coach telling him I had a better future in tennis."

Malaga was spectacularly prescient.

After obtaining his law degree from Western Reserve University, the streetwise young lawyer was on a political fast track. Before he turned 30 he was an assistant Ohio attorney general and an aide to Ohio Republican Governor C. William O'Neill.

At the same time he was active in Cleveland's somnolent tennis community. He seemed to be the only one awake and he let everyone know that, which led him to the presidency of the Northeast Ohio Tennis Association. He didn't run for the office. He was drafted and he took the job seriously.

Malaga began to lure minor international tennis events to Cleveland. In 1960 he secured rights to the Davis Cup Zone match between the United States and Venezuela with all the matches played at the Cleveland Skating Club on Kemper Road in Shaker Heights. He brought zone matches to Cleveland again in 1961 and '62. In those three years the United States Davis Cup team played Venezuela, Mexico and Canada, all at the Skating Club. The budgets for those events were humble. There was no television income. The only out-of-town newspapers that paid any attention were the New York Times and the Boston Globe. Malaga pulled it together by organizing an army of volunteers, including families who hosted players in their homes.

In 1963 he further dressed up our sporting calendar with the Wightman Cup matches, a traditional international event featuring the American women against the British women. As usual, it was held at the Skating Club.

When the United States won the Davis Cup in 1963, we also

earned the right to host the world finals the following year. Actually, world finals was not the term used at that time. The proper terminology was Challenge Round. By whatever name, however, Malaga went after it. Many people believed that stealing the Davis Cup from Forest Hills on Long Island, New York, was unrealistic. Forest Hills was intrinsic to American tennis in the way the Vatican is connected to Catholicism. They are one and the same. It was universally assumed that when the United States hosted the venerable Davis Cup Challenge Round, the matches would be held at Forest Hills—America's tennis capital. That was the case in the other years when the United States was in the host position. It was virtually automatic. It was a New York birthright.

But there was no rubber stamp in 1964. When the United States Lawn Tennis Association—the governing body of amateur tennis in this country—chose the location for the Davis Cup Challenge Round, it had three choices. Cleveland and Los Angeles bid for it, along with the traditional favorite New York.

The Los Angeles group was impressive, led by Perry Jones and his famous Los Angeles Tennis Club along with support from Pancho Gonzales and the City of Los Angeles.

Malaga, however, came in with an astounding cash guarantee of $100,000 to the United States Lawn Tennis Association.

The New York group rested on its laurels.

The decision was in the hands of the various tennis districts across the country. It went to a vote. After the first ballot the third-place finisher would drop out, which happened to be Los Angeles. That left Cleveland and New York.

Malaga went to work. He lobbied for votes from other Midwest districts. He called Los Angeles and said, "Do you really want Forest Hills to get this again?" Malaga's campaign came right off the streets of Collinwood.

New York was complacent. They were still sitting smugly on their hands when the votes were counted and Cleveland won.

Malaga next came face to face with that old expression, "Be careful what you wish for, you might get it."

He had the Davis Cup—which he renamed the Davis Cup World Finals—and he had no place to play it, among about a hundred other things he didn't have, including the hundred grand he had guaranteed to the USLTA.

Number one on his "to do" list was a venue. He needed somewhere to build an outdoor tennis stadium seating about 5,000 people. The World Finals were too big for the Skating Club. He got out a map looking for empty spaces. "This looks interesting," he said, pointing to the parking lot at Roxboro Junior High School in Cleveland Heights. He had a financial angel named Harold T. Clark whose name was attached to the tennis stadium which wasn't built yet. So Malaga struck a deal with the Cleveland Heights school board, which cobbled together bleachers from nearby baseball diamonds until they totaled about 5,000 seats, and then he was in business. This was a good deal for the Cleveland Heights schools. They got publicity, good will, rental income and summer jobs for their teenagers.

Cleveland always has benefited from an amazing community of volunteers and general do-gooders, and they came stampeding to the aid of the Davis Cup.

When it was over, Cleveland was acclaimed for the most successful Davis Cup World Finals ever held, except for the fact that Australia beat the United States and won back the Cup. Malaga went on to stage three more Davis Cup World Finals (1969, '70 and '73), three more Davis Cup Zone matches and five more Wightman Cup matches.

His greatest triumph, however, was none of these. He created a tournament in 1972 called the Bonne Bell Cup for the single purpose of a match between America's tennis sweetheart Chris Evert and the Australian star Evonne Goolagong. Evert was the top-ranked woman in the world and Goolagong was not far behind. They had never met.

"The matches were sold out, 5,000 seats, and there was still a demand for tickets," recalled Leon Blazey Jr., the Arthur Andersen CPA who handled the books for the Northeastern Ohio Tennis Association. "Bob looked at the bleachers and said, 'We could sell more tickets.' He did. He increased the seating capacity to 7,000.

"The night before the big match, he hired a bunch of kids to repaint and renumber the benches in two of the three sections. They reduced the width of each seat from 24 inches to 18 inches. It was suggested that some people would have a problem squeezing into 18 inches. 'Only fat-ass people are going to have a problem with that,' Malaga said. 'Let a fat-ass sit next to a skinny person.'

"Of course, the tickets had to be reprinted. The next day people were lined up as far as the eye could see and the printer hadn't finished running them off. Finally, he ran them to the box office. He had to sneak in the back door to the ticket office. If people knew he had all those tickets in his briefcase he never would have made it through the crowd.

"It turned out to be a very humid night and the paint didn't dry," Blazey continued. "One guy said he really enjoyed the matches, but he wondered what that was on his pants. He stood up and he had two stripes and the number '32' on the seat of his pants. After that we went back to 24-inch seats."

The following year another ticket problem was discovered at the Davis Cup World Finals, which were held indoors at Cleveland Public Hall.

"We sold the same seats twice," said Blazey. "Just like that, he came up with a solution. The first person to arrive got the seat. We moved the second person to the floor. We told them we were moving them to 'better seats' on the floor. Bob had a lot of guts. He liked a challenge."

For more than a decade Cleveland was called the tennis capital of the country and the USLTA, the governing body of tennis in this country, hired Malaga as its executive director, operating out of Cleveland.

For most of his working career he was one of four partners in a downtown law firm. One partner was dead, another rarely came to work, another drank and Malaga was the fourth, and most of his time was spent on tennis business. There were two secretaries, one shared by the partners who hardly worked and the second for Malaga.

Malaga also served for 18 months as a Cleveland Municipal Housing Court Judge. He served as a judge on Cuyahoga County Probate Court. He was executive director of the Lottery. But his heart had only one true love—tennis.

At the end of his life, Malaga was irascible, especially on his third vodka martini on the rocks with a twist. He never married and for many years lived in an apartment at Bratenahl Place, a high rise not far from the Collinwood neighborhood where he grew up. By the time he was 87 he had difficulty getting around and usually used a wheelchair.

His enduring hero was Sherlock Holmes. Once a week Malaga would watch a Sherlock Holmes television show in Blazey's TV room and invariably he would fall asleep. When the show was over, Malaga would wake up and Blazey would drive him home. Malaga's parting words never varied.

"Sherlock always gets his man," he would say.

Gratitudes

To THOSE WHO MADE contributions to this book:

Joe Smith for endless suggestions and encouragement

Albert Belle, may his afterlife be marked by hot coals and sulphurous fumes

Bill Hickey for writing the greatest football novel of all time

Wally Pisorn for hiring gorgeous bartenders

Neil Zurcher for Jim Fixx

Bob Gain for uttering those magic words, "Shoot me."

Dave Plagman for Gary Dee

Mike Holland and Russ Carson for Otto Graham

Jack Herrick and Lee Blazey for Bob Malaga

Kent Schneider for Ted Stepien

Bob Stewart for Canton McKinley

David Dwoskin for the real Stadium Mustard

Frank Borroni and Tom Hatfield for soccer literature

Larry Chernauskas for basketball 101

Jim Mueller for humbling Humble Howie

The BottleHouse Brewing Company for providing the location for the cover photograph.

John Luttermoser for copy editing

About the Author

Dan Coughlin has covered the Cleveland sports scene for 45 years as a newspaperman, magazine writer, television broadcaster and radio commentator. He was twice named Ohio sportswriter of the year and was honored with a television Emmy. He traveled with both the Cleveland Browns and Indians. He covered some of the biggest college football games of the 20th century, including five major bowl games. As a boxing writer he was at ringside for several world championship fights as well as the Muhammad Ali and Joe Frazier series. He covered 17 Indianapolis 500s and several auto races in Europe. While in college he broadcast Notre Dame basketball and baseball games on the student radio station.

Dan served his alma mater, St. Edward High School, as a member of its board of trustees for 20 years. Because of his generosity, several bartenders were able to send their sons to St. Edward. He is a member of the Greater Cleveland Softball Hall of Fame and the Press Club of Cleveland Hall of Fame, and he is a past president of the Press Club. He now lives in Rocky River, Ohio, with his wife, Maddy.